The Unspoken Gospel

The Unspoken Gospel

Living Faith Beyond Borders

By
Ellen Janzen

MOF Publishing

MOF PUBLISHING

MOF PUBLISHING MOF Publishing

The Unspoken Gospel: Living Faith Beyond Borders

paperback edition © March 2018: ISBN 978-0-9958951-3-3

Requests for information should be addressed to:
MOF Publishing
mofpublishing@proinbox.com

Janzen, Ellen, 1961-, author
The unspoken gospel: living faith beyond borders

Issued in print and electronic formats.
ISBN 978-0-9958951-3-3 (softcover).--ISBN 978-0-9958951-4-0(HTML)
1. Janzen, Ellen, 1961-. 2. Autobiographies. I. Title

Cover design: Ellen Janzen

Interior design & composition: Ellen Janzen

Printed in Canada.

In loving memory of Granny Meri,
who sang her songs daily
and
Teaches my heart
about heaven and home,
still.

Table of Contents

Acknowledgements

It takes a lot of courage to write a book and put it out into the public eye. More courage than I possess. So I gratefully acknowledge and thank all the friends who gave me courage—some just by throwing a tiny pebble at my window, so I would open that window and let in a fresh breeze. Others by creating a manufacturing plant of encouragement and sending generous shipments my way. You all held me to the task and helped me finish—I hope well.

You are, to name a few (and no doubt miss a few)—
Pam, Sue, Tami, Amy, Alice, John, AJ, Karen, Grace, Betsy, Mel, Tracey, Rose, Mary. Sandra: generous shipments.

For Val, whose kindness in editing makes me want to write more clearly. You gently challenge my thinking to a higher level. And those sharp eyes that catch my every mistake. Grateful beyond words, I truly am.

And my friends of other names, but here recorded as Selma, Naima, Meriem, Esma, Faith, Hejer...and many more, un-named, most especially "Jim's wife." You taught me to love your country and culture and to see the world a new way. Thank you for your patience and inclusion, which contributed so much to the transforming work of God in my life.

AJ—always and ever the best for me in every way.

Introduction

We all grow up inside the bubble of *culture*. It shapes the way we express our values—what is right and wrong, polite and impolite, favourable or inappropriate. We live by values and customs that are agreed upon and shared but rarely talked about explicitly. Under normal circumstances these conventions become a part of who we are without consciously being learned.

They are everywhere implied but never openly declared, to borrow a phrase from an English novelist, Jane Austen.

Unless the bubble bursts. This happens when our expectations are not met—when we interact with people whose behaviours don't fit into our paradigm. We begin to recognize, sometimes amidst chaos, that there are ways to view the world other than what was around us as we grew up. Culture is like a window for viewing life.

Culture has the power to create camaraderie and build community by influencing what we value and what we don't tolerate within silent boundaries. Outside those boundaries, culture has equal power to cause misunderstandings, fracture affiliations, or create barriers. Across the world there are thousands of cultures—each one valuable and unique. How do we unravel the distinctions and understand the differences?

For 150 years Canada has integrated diverse cultures into the fabric of a growing nation. This millennium has seen that diversity increase. Where previously the foreign-born population came primarily from Europe, there have been two major changes since 2000. The percentage of Canadians who are foreign born has grown from about 11-15% before 2000 to over 20% in 2011. That year, over 6.7 million Canadians were first generation immigrants. The second change has been in countries of origin. They are now largely Asian rather than European, representing a significant shift in culture.[1] The escalation of conflict in parts of the world since 2011 has increased the number of refugees coming to Canada. Amazingly, the rate of cultural adaptation is increasing, not stabilizing, but that is part of who we are as Canadians.

---

[1] *Statistics Canada, "150 Years of Immigration in Canada," (http://www.statcan.gc.ca/pub/11-630-x/11-630-x2016006-eng.htm, 2018).*

As people from new nations join us, they each bring a unique worldview and culture—and let's be real, "we", the European settlers of this vast land, have not been here all that long. Most of our families have been Canadian for four or five generations. As this migration affects us, our country becomes a wider mix of varying world views. This holds the potential for a richer, broader culture.

The culture of the West was formed fairly recently under the pressures of the Industrial Revolution in Britain. Reliance on machines replaced work people had done, moving life away from relationships that focused on community. Individualism took over. Then during the World Wars, women moved into work places in large numbers and their focus on home and family shifted toward a greater focus on earning incomes. A growing desire or need for double incomes meant less time spent together as a family unit. This further moved the culture toward an individualistic orientation.

At about the same time, Western education turned to rational thought and scientific study as the primary means of pursuing truth. By contrast, Eastern cultures maintained a focus on community and family. These traditional values still shape many cultures, particularly those from Asia, but also including Africa and Latin America.

I refer to "traditional cultures" as an inclusive term for many of the cultures found in Asia, Africa, the global South, or even rural cultures. It is a term I learned studying with a Canadian professor of developmental psychology, Dr. Gordon Neufeld.[2]

One of the distinctives of traditional culture is that our human intuition has a role in guiding behaviour. With less focus on scientific research and rational explanation, life is understood from the standpoint of instinct and intuition—the inner drive or "voice" that we trust to guide us.

Sometimes our intuition warns of danger and we register alarm, taking steps to be cautious as a result. Sometimes it presents in how we "read" people—noting unconsciously their posture or eye movements. These instincts are within us for a reason—they are part of our survival systems. But to survive we need to live in "herds"—connected to others for our protection and provision—the give and take of community. Relationships thrive more fully when human intuition is considered credible.[3] Community flourishes when we follow the instinctive need to

---

[2] *Gordon Neufeld, Neufeld Intensive 1: Making Sense of Kids, course (Neufeld Institute, Vancouver, BC, 2015), http://neufeldinstitute.org/course/neufeld-intensive-i-making-sense-of-kids/.*

[3] *Gordon Neufeld, Neufeld Intensive I, 2015.*

connect and care for each other. People from traditional cultures bring these values with them and contribute them to Canadian society.

As we accept our expanding weave as a Canadian culture, it is important to take the time to welcome and understand our newest citizens. They have valuable things to teach us, if we are willing to learn. And we bear the responsibility of helping new Canadians understand who we are—for their sake as well as our own.

Why is it our responsibility? For starters, if we are following the instruction of Scripture, this is what is taught there.

Do not mistreat or oppress a foreigner, for you were foreigners in Egypt. Exodus 22:21

He defends the cause of the fatherless and the widow, and loves the foreigner residing among you, giving them food and clothing. Deuteronomy 10:18

Cursed is anyone who withholds justice from the foreigner, the fatherless or the widow. Deuteronomy 27:19

Secondly, if we don't want our country fractured into categories of "them and us" (which can lead to breakdown and even violence), we need to take the lead and invite relationship with newcomers. We need to participate in weaving the fabric together.

And thirdly, it weighs on our humanity and compassion to be the ones to reach out and initiate understanding. The winds of change that are shifting world population are so often the stormy gale of upheaval. When newcomers are victims of war and violence, running for the sake of saving their children's lives, they are not necessarily going to realize it is their responsibility to learn the new culture and adapt to it. Fear takes precedence where common sense might have normally prevailed. Rational observations of social expectations that are different and possibly demanding might be missed due to PTSD (post-traumatic stress disorder). If trauma with its ugly nightmares has chased newcomers here, then it is not fair for us to place high expectations on them to initiate friendships with strangers. We should not demand that immigrants learn a new set of "manners" along with all that it takes to survive before we will befriend them.

What is daunting about this task is that it invites the inevitability of mistakes. It feels like a huge risk, *because it is.* Probably we will miss things. Probably we will offend. Probably we will feel the pain of being inadequate at one point or another.

On the other hand—and with risk there is always the "other hand"—the benefits are impressive. We will learn about grace, about ourselves, about our faith, and we will become a better expression of the God who redeems—the Gospel message is at the heart of this endeavour.

I tell my stories in the hope that they will give you insight as well as courage. You—and what I know about you is that you have opened these pages to read about offering kindness to a newcomer—have so much to offer. Your interest, your time, your willingness to journey beside someone from a far-off land, is a blessing without boundaries...the limits are only there if you put them there.

In case you think I have forgotten, let me say that what applies to this topic of new Canadians, most of whom have traditional (non-Western) cultural values, also applies to the traditional cultures that were in this land before we (the Westerners) arrived. So maybe, just maybe, we are in the process of restoring the culture to where it needs to be.

In my first year after I returned to live in Canada, the most common question I was asked was how to befriend new Canadians from Eastern countries. Recognizing that each country has its own culture and that many of these values play out in different customs even within the same country, I offer the insights as broad strokes. You have to get to know families if you want to understand how their cultures see things—this book is just a starting point.

In these stories I hope you will find helpful insights. I hope you will have courage as you read about how I blundered through many situations, to reach out and get to know women and their families who carry the values of traditional culture—and become their friend.

~ 1 ~

Friendship is Not a Job

It is no use walking anywhere to preach
unless our walking is our preaching.
Francis of Assisi

With my baby gently nodding his head inside my blue corduroy snuggly and my four-year-old daughter chatting easily beside me, I had a choice to make. Should we walk on the sunny side of the street, or stay in the shade?

It was a seven-minute walk to the *dukan*—the little shop where our family could buy sugar, flour, salt, tomato paste, and candy. We wished we could get powdered milk and yogurt here, like we had seen in the capital city when we arrived. Our city had no luxuries, so we had exciting plans to make a crazy chocolate cake—the kind that fizzed with soda and vinegar. But we needed sugar, which required a welcome walk to the "sugar shop"—our own name for the *dukan.*

If I chose the sunny side of the street, I knew we would soon be taking off our scarves and jackets, and we would be too hot by the time we got to the *dukan*. The baby would fuss in the too-warm confines of the snuggly. But if we stayed in the shade, we would barely enjoy the walk, with the lingering shards of the desert night cold stabbing at our fingers and noses. This discrepancy between the hot and cold of sun and shade reminded me of my mom talking about the *altiplano*—the desert in Chile and Bolivia in South America where I had grown up.

"No wonder they worship the sun," Mom had observed. "The minute the sun goes down, you feel as if you are going to freeze." The shade on the *altiplano* felt just like this winter shade—stabbing at our extremities with a cruel chill.

It was my first month of living in the Sahara region of North Africa. Who knew winter could be this cold here? As we walked toward the sugar shop, I mused on all the experiences of my life that had prepared me for this city.

Turning a corner I spotted a woman standing in the edge of her doorway, or rather the door of the wall that surrounded her front yard. High cement walls, all painted white, prevented us from seeing into anyone's property. These yards were cleaned each morning by ambitious housewives, determined to keep the Sahara sand from overtaking their homes. It was quite common to catch a glimpse of a woman standing in her doorway, catching a few rays of the warming sun. If she ducked inside and closed the metal door just as we turned onto her street, I knew she didn't want to talk to us. But more often than not, a woman standing there would watch us walk past—we were, admittedly, a unique sight in this neighbourhood, almost as fun as having Martians arrive.

At first I had thought these housewives were unfriendly, their faces were always a mask of—of what? For the first two weeks, the mask had looked suspicious and surly to my Western eyes. But I'd come to see this expression as one of uncertainty—they didn't know what to make of me and were guarded. Until I broke the ice with a simple greeting.

When I began saying, "*Salamu 'alaykum*" to each woman I passed, I quickly learned two things. The mask was a thin veil that was instantly replaced by a broad smile and a flash of delight in response to my greeting. Additionally, if I was willing to stop and converse, I would inevitably be invited in for coffee and cookies. This invitation could save us the need to eat cake, but that would also disappoint my daughter who loved the mixing and stirring as well as her brothers who preferred the eating part!

Apart from this one housewife standing in her doorway, the street would be empty all the way to the *dukan* and back on most days. Women didn't walk on the street without a man to escort them, even to a neighbour's for tea. This made us a curiosity, and perhaps the intrigue motivated their invitation for us to visit. The times when we chose to push the first domino by giving a greeting and then accepting the opened door, we found the welcome was genuine.

We would share in our limited Arabic where we had come from and who the members of our family were. This was how we began to learn the culture of the people of this city. The invitation consistently began with the offer of coffee with a sweet treat as the offer of food was embedded into an invitation to a friendship. And the welcome was always as warm as the sunshine on the "right" side of the street.

We also got invited home by many of my husband's students, where an elaborate meal was followed by 4 or 5 hours of visiting. It would have been unthinkable to invite us home and not offer a meal, but I often felt unnecessary in a visit made alongside of my husband. He knew enough local language to carry on a conversation, and I would just listen, silently. In the evenings, more often than not, when we were invited home to meet a student's family, I was ushered through the house to a women's group in a back room where conversation was optional. My silence was accepted and ignored in this setting. The men gathered in the front living room often engrossed in a boisterous discussion until well past midnight. I would resort to sending my son down the hallway to find his dad and carry the message—"Mama wants to go home now."

These long visits, uncluttered by conversation (on my part), gave me time to observe and contemplate. I began to pick up that there were subtle messages in the women's interactions. My silence made me more aware of the innuendos, and I recognized that there were other women who were watching silently—taking in the unspoken messages. One of my devotional reflections led me to verses that became obligingly instructive in this new setting.

Adopt the same attitude as that of Christ Jesus,
who, existing in the form of God,
did not consider equality with God
as something to be exploited.
Instead he emptied himself
by assuming the form of a servant,
taking on the likeness of humanity. Philippians 2:5-7 CSB.

I began to comprehend that although I couldn't converse well with the women, they were observing actions and conversations between me and my children. The presence of Christ in my life—the Gospel message itself—was not a set of words or theological propositions and certainly not an apologetic argument, given my linguistic stumbles. In this setting, the Gospel message—the heart of God's love for the lost—was conveyed in the way I chose to relate non-verbally with the women and in my relationship with my children.

The love of a redeeming God could not be explained but it could be seen—this was an insight that would compel me to care for my family well and show kindness to those whose lives I touched. For the next twenty years, this tension between words and truth, explanation and expression, continued to challenge me, even after I was more conversant in the local dialect.

One of the keys to "living" the Gospel without words, I discovered, was that I needed to fill the cultural gap between East and West with understanding—my own understanding of the differences. It was essential that I learn to see things through another window, framed by humility, that would allow me to loosen my interpretation of what was of value in how things were done. It wasn't that I had to agree with the conclusions drawn by that "new" perspective, but I needed to at least recognize that my way wasn't necessarily the "right" way. It definitely wasn't the *only* way.

I would learn that even 30 miles down the road in another village, things might be done yet differently again—it was about looking beyond the details and seeing the values as well as the customs and protocols. For instance, how one showed hospitality would vary from place to place, but the value on being hospitable was distinctly more important than what we held to in Canada.

Sometimes things were said or done in a way that I found abrupt and aggressive but no offense was intended. Likewise, my ways of being polite or showing respect didn't always convey my intentions. I understood how to express love and respect in my home culture, and I needed to learn the social cues to convey these in a culture that had completely different traditions.

I needed to learn how to embrace friendship inside a new set of cultural norms and practices. I watched Westerners around me build friendships where all their needs were met by each other. Only a few expats made the effort to create deeply meaningful relationships with their neighbours where they shared their needs and were vulnerable—as a friend.

It was hard to jump the chasm that lay between the Western cultures familiar to us and the Eastern culture we lived in. I found that leap uncomfortable, feeling precarious as I wondered where I would land. I persisted by telling myself I had tolerance for chaos and ambiguity. Local women seemed to yearn for friendship, even though how they expressed this was sometimes puzzling and paradoxical.

As I made an effort to learn more about the impact of culture on friendship, I found myself invigorated. The opportunity to assimilate into my local, host culture this way was engaging, life-giving. One lady I met briefly challenged me with a single phrase: "Friendship isn't a job." I couldn't make friends by choosing to treat people as if I had to get to know them or be their friend. If I wanted genuine relationship I had to give it from the vulnerability of my own soul. Women from the local culture could tell when I was being genuine, giving my "best" to the friendship. It was a matter of feeding it with the right nutrients.

We cultivate plants with good soil, enough sun, clean water, and the right plant food so that we can confidently expect them to flourish. The same can be done for friendships. And just as transplanted shrubs need that careful attention in order to take root, friendships between cultures need special attention, too. The more specific support you give them, the more likely they are to flourish.

I was learning to be a good gardener in this, my new "front yard" where the blooms were not always what I expected and sometimes each seed needed slightly different care. There were plenty of days when I felt the hot scorching sun of the desert and longed for the cooler gardens of "home." But I had been told that my tenacious character would stand me in good stead on this adventure—and as the years passed, I saw myself changing and learning.

TIPS, SUGGESTIONS AND QUESTIONS:

What, in your understanding are the basic, guiding values of your heart culture? One of the things that interactions with other cultures will give you back as a gift is a greater ability to see what you value. When you meet people from other cultures are you able to see what they value?

When it comes to learning about a new culture, the easiest mistake we can make is in the interpretation of other's actions—can you see that in the story of the walk to the *dukan*? It is a skill and a discipline to catch this in yourself and to start with curiosity that will lead you to ask what you might not be understanding accurately.

What are the cultures that have contributed to how you do things—what you value and how you live out those values? What are some things you might be curious about from other cultures? When you see someone whose dress suggests they are new to this country, is there an expression on their face that you are interpreting—or misinterpreting? What do you think it is? What else might it be?

As you think about this, you might want to start making a list of different ways you have observed these differences and how you have interpreted them—do you think of certain cultures as "emotional" or "rude"? How could curiosity and questions help you revisit those ideas and understand them differently?

One of the best ways to be genuine with someone is to ask them to actually teach you something—how to cook their food, or make something by hand. In turn this empowers them as a teacher and helps them feel less insecure about themselves. Sometimes silence is just another cover for a lack of confidence.

QUESTIONS FOR REFLECTION:

Can you think of a time in your life when you felt God asked you to participate in the verses from Philippians 2:5-7—pouring out your own self in order to meet the needs of others? Or, how might pouring yourself out be expressed by *having* a need? Is this part of what Jesus did? How might this be a central issue if you want to pursue a relationship with someone from another culture?

From Susan—on the learning curve in Rwanda:

I remember my early days in Rwanda, trying to make eye contact with people I would pass on the street. I would look at people and smile at them, hoping they would return the gesture. More often than not, the Rwandese would just stare at me, not smile. They didn't seem interested in knowing me or acknowledging me at all. It was discouraging.

I'm sure it was God who finally gave me the clarity on what I was doing incorrectly. Thankfully. I realized, by watching the locals greet one another, that they had a distinct way of making eye contact. I had missed it. When greeting a Rwandese, it is important to give a slight raise of your head, while raising your eyebrows at the same time as you make eye contact.

It worked like magic! The first time I tested it out, I was stunned to have the same gesture returned, along with a bright smile and greeting. It wasn't that they didn't like me or want to know me, they just didn't understand me. Once I figured out how to do things their way, a whole new world opened up. I became so accustomed to raising my eyebrows all the time, that when we returned to Canada I did the same to my Canadian friends. They must have thought I was strange. It took a while to break that habit. Ha!

It was so important for me to enter my new culture as a humble learner, observer and listener.

~ 2 ~

Food is our First Love Language

Cooking is love
made edible.
Michael Mullan

When we cross cultural boundaries, either by moving overseas or by making friends with someone from another background, we instinctively look for things we understand. Human instincts have one main purpose—to build relationships that serve community. Survival instincts may be shaped by culture, but all humans have them. And although they may be more easily observed in children, they work for the same purpose in adults. We need to be connected to each other in order to survive.

Babies are wired for connection and relationship, starting with their first cry for food. These cries, along with how a newborn's five senses work, draw the baby and the mother together in order to provide for the infant's primary needs for safety, warmth, and milk. We need more than food to survive, but as a crucial piece of the puzzle, human instincts push us toward safety by using our need for food. Safety and nourishment are bound together by a vital relationship between parent and child that develops and matures over the first decades of life.[4]

The survival instinct that binds food to a safe, comforting relationship is unconsciously understood in the traditional cultures of the world, but nowhere more than in the desert. When nomads living in the desert see

---

[4] *Margie S Deutsch Lash, Nancy Williams, Gretchen Andrews and Shawn Crane, Stone Age Baby in a Techno Society (N.p.: CreateSpace Independent Publishing Platform, 2012).*

travellers approaching, there is a deep understanding that hospitality is life-giving. To withhold food and water from travellers would be unimaginable and uncivilized—"ill-bred."

Being regarded as "ill-bred" is not a searing insult in our culture, but in some cultures it would be a shocking affront to even say this word to a person's face. If a person is ill-bred, it implies he or she is from "bad stock"—the reputation of the entire family is called into question by one unsavoury member. This brings shame rather than honour on the family. Within the culture, family honour dictates many decisions that are made.

Honour is profoundly important as a cultural value, so much so that some anthropologists classify cultures as shame-based or shame vs. honour cultures. At the heart of this value is the issue of hospitality which goes hand in hand with good breeding—because it represents the preservation of life. In traditional cultures, any relationship of good repute begins with the giving and receiving of hospitality.

For a long time after I arrived in North Africa, I looked to questions and conversation as the beginning of a friendship even though I knew this was not the main thing I saw around me. After some years, the importance of hospitality, even between strangers in public spaces, started to make sense and sink in to affect my soul.

The introductory conversation about names, nationalities, and life circumstances is just a knock on the door. To open the door of friendship, we need a message that "sings" of welcome. For many cultures, that is a song without lyrics. It is innuendo and rhythm and harmony—but not words. You don't *tell* someone that you care about them—you show them, with hospitality.

I made a trip from North Africa to Canada by myself one winter, leaving my children at home with their capable dad. I was "Footloose and fancy free" as my mother would have described it, getting on the minibus at 7:00 am for a two hour ride to the capital city. I sat next to a young woman who chatted easily and shared about her life as a university student. I knew enough about the university and people there to ask the right questions. We were "getting along famously" (another of my mom's sayings) when she opened her bag and pulled out a local chocolate bar.

Because we had been chatting already, I knew immediately that I was going to be offered a piece of chocolate—it would have been unthinkable for her to eat it in front of me without holding it out for me to take some. Normally I would enjoy receiving a piece of chocolate but not before 8:00 am.

I calculated the effect of saying "No, thank you," to her. It would dampen the joy we were generating in getting to know each other. Culturally, refusing food held within it the implication that I was not interested in a friendship—something we wouldn't even notice in our Western culture. I could circumvent this by saying, "I'm sorry, chocolate isn't good for my health"—she might know it was an excuse but would still respect that I was not rejecting her offer. Despite understanding this part of the culture, it felt untruthful to say this. My options flashed through my mind as she opened the wrapper and held it toward me in a generous invitation to join her in a breakfast treat.

I ate the chocolate, and our camaraderie grew warmer as the morning sun rose. By the time we parted, her good-bye included a warm kiss to each of my cheeks, evoking a tender satisfaction inside of me. The way she said good-bye told me, "Thank you for being my friend." Though it was a short friendship, it had brought us both delight. We had made the journey rich with companionship for each other.

I made it to London, late by about two hours. My transit time was fraught with panic as I ran through the airport and waited in long security lines, arriving at my next gate frazzled and tired. I had skipped the luxury of buying a sandwich in the time crunch. Now I was well and truly hungry.

I buckled myself into my seat next to another young woman, and we politely introduced ourselves. She was also a university student, reserved in a different way than my first companion. I was not as comfortable with the barriers in the British culture, so we didn't make it past the polite introductions. Then she pulled out a chocolate bar—not just any chocolate bar, but a coveted Cadbury's milk chocolate (probably with nuts—my favourite). I wanted a piece of that chocolate in the worst way. It was about four in the afternoon, and I had missed lunch—now was the perfect time for a "little something."

Yet I knew I wasn't going to be offered a morsel. Giving chocolate to strangers in England is not normal. I contemplated asking for a piece, but my Canadian reserve held me back. In North Africa, the boldness of asking for a piece of chocolate would have been honoured with ease and grace. But in this pristine row of a British Airways jetliner, I knew it would sound brash and pushy—my Canadian soul retreated into a polite, hungry silence.

Not surprisingly, when we said our good-byes at the end of our journey, there was a courteous but stilted distance between us. We had not crossed any barriers, and the warm satisfaction of having contributed to a temporary connection was vaguely missing. Shared food that could have offered the connective tissue of interest and care had been consumed by only one of us. She probably had other priorities on the trip—as I often do.

As a Westerner, I rarely look for a connection with people I sit beside on public transport—I relish the silence as time to listen to music and read a book I have selected. But I learned from my time overseas that there is a worthy gift in such an encounter. It is the gift of being seen—of being acknowledged and invited into someone else's journey. This may be fleeting and inconsequential, or it may change my entire experience. If I am sitting beside someone from another culture, I usually assume there will be a better connection if I offer them something to eat—a travel candy is usually accepted by Westerners.

There are five love languages common to Eastern (and traditional) cultures, in my experience. They are food, food, food, time$^{\mathbf{2}}$, and touch. Food is the all important first one. If you skip over this and don't offer anything to a guest, you are, to quote Nanny (from *Eloise at the Plaza)*, "Rude, rude, rude."[5]

Time is viewed quite differently in traditional cultures than it is in the West. It is something you give to people, to honour them. In my estimation, you should multiply your expectations and give your time exponentially—if you expect that three hours is long enough for a visit or social event, I would guesstimate that the recipient might be hoping for nine hours (three squared).

And touch is taken for granted as the way you will express your interest in someone—you don't talk about what they mean to you, you kiss cheeks, touch their hand, or link arms. Different countries and cultures will have differences in how they express this. But generally the reserve we feel about our personal space in Western cultures is misunderstood as disinterest. You show your kindness and concern by reaching into someone's space and connecting. The expression of this will vary from place to place, so this has to be observed to be learned.

Food, and how it invites connection, is the first doorway to notice and understand. In most traditional cultures, food or drink is not offered with words but by putting it down in front of you. You are not obligated to eat everything you are offered, but no one asks first if you want something. Western culture has a verbal approach, asking if someone wants what is on offer. To an Easterner this may sound like you don't really want to

---

[5] *Kay Thomson and Hilary Knight, Eloise at the Plaza (New York: Little Simon, 1955).*

bother, so they will say "no" to the first offer, checking to see if you really mean it. You have to offer a second or even a third time.

The instinct that responds to an offer of food and other physical care is the deepest of all instincts, and it is valued in many traditional cultures, as I described in the chocolate I was offered on that early morning trip. Instinctively we feel cared for when someone gives us food or drink, even if we aren't hungry.

But this is not the only instinct that leads us toward friendship. Friendships grow if we pay attention to the instincts we have to connect—again, these are rarely described but they are the ever-present influences that give us a sense of being "on the right track."

TIPS, SUGGESTIONS AND QUESTIONS:

When it comes to stepping out of your comfort zone to create a friendship with someone from another country, the offer of food is one of the safest places to start (but research if there are "forbidden" foods—such as pork for Muslims). Try to include hospitality and the offer of food into the beginning stages of a friendship in some way. If you are eating around someone of another culture, you can politely offer some of what you have—their response will tell you what food values their culture has. If you have neighbours from another country on your street, bring them a plate of cookies or a bowl of grapes. If you don't bake, make the effort to get something at a nice bakery. This says more than a packet of generic chocolate chip cookies. In some cultures, a well-wrapped box of chocolates is the best gift to offer. Sometimes the wrapping is more important than the gift inside—fancy wrapping is a message, even to our Western eyes.

I would be very surprised if any new neighbours from a traditional culture that you give something to don't return the invitation in some way—and this will give you the opportunity to understand what an open door looks like to them. Watch and see how people from a traditional culture invite you into their lives. If food is not the very first expression of their care and desire for you to be a part of their life, then they have probably made a conscious effort to adapt to our Western ways or have lived here a long time. Even then, I would be surprised if they could separate food from friendship.

If you are invited to a friend's home for a meal, I would say it is important to err on the side of caution and bring a gift—either of food to share or a plant or something similar. This may not be "required" in every culture, but it is better to be too generous than to bring nothing when a gift would be considered "normal."

Very commonly, there are also traditional sayings or greetings that surround the offer of food and its consumption. If you don't have an opportunity to observe these greetings between people of another culture then it is something you could simply ask about. You might ask, "Do you have something you say every time you eat together, or when you are finished eating?" Learning these little phrases will move you into a new level of friendship quite quickly.

If you offer food or drink—tea or coffee—to someone and they decline in a way that indicates they don't want to be a bother, you are probably safe to assume that their answer actually means "Yes." This is a risk well worth taking—giving the offered item when the answer sounds dubious. I would say this is also true for most of my Western guests.

Here are a few things to avoid: don't bring your own coffee or water bottle over to a neighbour's house thinking she will feel like you have done her a favour! She will likely interpret this action as meaning that you don't trust her water or like her coffee. Don't tell her, "Oh, you shouldn't have," if she offers you food and drink—but tell her how honoured you feel to be treated so well. This is what she is doing—she is honouring you. Don't outright refuse anything she offers unless there is medical reason, but if you can't eat it all, don't feel bad about that either. Even taking one bite or drinking one sip will show you are grateful, and you can offer the explanation that, "Sugar isn't good for me," or "I have to be careful for health reasons."

QUESTIONS FOR REFLECTION:

Can you think of a time when you were hungry or tired and someone offered you hospitality—food or refreshment or a place to rest—and that gift felt like it was "life-giving"? How did you feel toward the person who offered it as a result?

Can you see this theme of "life-giving hospitality" in the stories about Jesus? How did he use phrases about food and water in reference to his own identity?

***Maria, who is from the Philippines**, lived in Afghanistan for six years. Here are some of her observations on living cross culturally:*

Being Asian, I grew up in an honour and shame culture. A person's way of conducting themselves may put their reputation and, to a certain extent, the whole family's reputation at stake as well. That is why as much as possible in Afghanistan, I would try my best not to offend other people because it could affect my family's reputation. Also, for Filipinos and Afghans, even unpleasant news can be received very well when delivered and shared in a careful and polite manner; rather than a direct or frank way.

Though it is shameful to hurt other people's feelings, hurt does happen and conflicts do arise. In this case, we need, what Filipinos call, a "padrino," or a third party/person to mediate and somehow act as a witness. He/she must be someone considered honourable and respected in the clan or in a society. Likewise, we were very careful not to hurt and bring shame to Afghans. We also identified with the need for mediators to resolve certain issues.

Second, Filipino families are usually so close to one another that the house may include extended family members – grandparents, uncles, aunties and cousins. If one family member gets married, but is unable to have their own place yet, they are welcome to stay with the family until they are comfortable to live on their own.

Afghan families are big families too! Many live and function as one big extended family. Like the Filipinos, close family ties are valuable to them. At times, this meant that when we met with one Afghan family member, our whole family would be invited by the father or head of household to meet with the entire extended family. As Filipinos, we easily identified with the importance of the extended family.

~ 3 ~

Instincts: The Friendship Ladder

The language of Friendship
is not words but meanings.
Henry David Thoreau

Developmental psychologists study and observe human behaviour and make sense of the inner world that drives humans. Dr. Gordon Neufeld, a Canadian child psychologist, has assimilated studies from cultures across the world, noting that there is a hierarchy of instincts that carry children through their first five years of life. Each of these builds a stronger sense of connection for children with their family and "the village of attachment" around them.[6] These instincts, or "roots of attachment," are found across cultures. They continue to guide us as adults, so by knowing them we can give ourselves a map—a reference point for understanding how relationships grow.[7]

The primal instinct to connect and attach to those who meet a baby's physical needs (food, shelter, comfort) is followed by other observable instincts. These needs are usually signalled and met by using the five senses—sight, sound, touch, taste and smell, and are surprisingly well developed in newborn infants. Dr. Neufeld refers to these as instincts that cause us to ***come alongside*** each other.[8]

Toward the end of the first year of life, babies begin to copy the behaviour of those they trust, forming an ever-growing sense of connection. As children mimic facial expressions, sounds (language),

---

[6] *Gordon Neufeld and Gabor Mate, Hold on to your Kids (Toronto: Alfred A. Knopf, 2004).*

[7] *Neufeld, Neufeld Intensive 1, 2015.*

[8] *Neufeld, Neufeld Intensive 1, 2015.*

and reactions of pleasure and distaste, they begin to learn values from the people they copy. This inner desire to be alike never leaves us. As adults we instinctively connect to those who have behaviours, interests, or values similar to our own—this is the ***instinct for sameness.***

In our house, we often talk and laugh around the table at supper. We enjoyed watching our fifteen-month-old grandson as he learned the social behaviour of shared jokes from some of these times. He started laughing long and loud in order to join in the hilarity—before he had a clue why we laughed. When he started to throw his head back and look at the ceiling, we all realized which of us laughed this way. Next he clapped his hands over his mouth. We became aware of our gestures of merriment as he isolated and imitated them. Of course this made us laugh all the harder. It was a fun game! He was demonstrating his instinct to imitate the "village" of people he loved.

We often search in conversations for something we share in common with someone we meet. You may remember this moment in a romantic relationship, but it is everywhere. If you take the time to notice, there is a sense of being more settled, like a sigh of relief, in most conversations with strangers when you reach this point—almost like an "Ahhh. I've found what we can share together." Finding "sameness" is a second step up the ladder of friendship.

In the third year of life, a new instinct emerges: the ***instinct for belonging***. This sense of being one of the group leads the way in creating a sense of family connection and loyalty. It is that important piece of "team spirit" that tells us we are all on the same side. We don't forge deep relationships with people unless we feel they are working for us (not against us). For toddlers, this is what pushes them toward compliant behaviour because their instincts drive them to be "one of us." Some researchers call this "herd behaviour."

In Danish culture, a winter custom called "*hygge*" promotes this desire for belonging. There are always a few words in a language that are difficult to translate into other languages. *Hygge* is one of those words. It has been translated as "cozy," but its meaning is larger than that. It is the winter custom of enjoying cold weather as a gift that focuses family members on snuggling into a warm place together—present with one another. The activities of this ritual build awareness, conversation, and belonging.

Every healthy, happy family has a series of such rituals that give them a sense of being a team. They may be simple or elaborate, daily or seasonal, but they satisfy this instinct we have—the need to belong to each other. Often they cluster around holidays, like Christmas and Thanksgiving—we look forward to the familiar, fun activities that create belonging. We repeat these from year to year and they gather us back into a sense of "home"—family togetherness.

Our family rituals for our evening meal included putting a candle beside each plate and lighting it once we started eating. We had various songs we sang for grace and after dinner my husband read aloud to us. Outside of dinner time we had other rituals and favourite sayings that gave us a sense of belonging to each other.

As friendships form, these instincts for belonging drive us to find a groove—forming habits that give us a sense of being on the same side, with expectations for the next time we meet. They may be as uncomplicated as meeting at the same coffee shop, or they could be a love for hiking or a shared interest in a hobby. The sense of belonging, enjoying the same activities, knowing it will happen again—these come out of a human instinct for social behaviour and belonging.

I can trace that sense of belonging and identity in a number of singing groups from my college years. We had "in" jokes and sayings we could predict as part of our repartee, creating an identity between us. Laughter was the glue that made us feel like a team. For people who don't come from a family with a strong sense of belonging, perhaps the connection of *belonging* was found in some other kind of team such as sports or music.

For me, this sense of belonging to the new culture of North Africa was a struggle. It came much easier to my husband who loved the music, enjoyed social interactions, and learned the language easily. He took notice of all the local sayings and how they fit to different situations, and as he used them, he made people laugh. He had found his "place" in the culture. Although it took me longer, I eventually found what I loved in the sense of belonging and community.

As the stage of belonging matures, the next instinct emerges—the ***need for significance***. This stage builds on belonging but takes you beyond needing to fit in and find meaning in being one of the group. This instinct emerges as the *need to be unique*—to balance belonging with autonomy within that group. We all tend to grow into ourselves—become more fully who we are as an individual—when we find a group where we feel safe enough to try things that make us feel vulnerable. This kind of group connects stability and acceptance with uniqueness and self-expression. We need both to grow into a full expression of our identity.

The stage of *significance* comes in any relationship when we disagree or have our own point of view but still feel respected and valued. If a friendship does not progress to this stage, it will usually break down or fizzle out. A friendship that requires perfect agreement has an element that usually feels fake—it is not one we expect to last through hard times. Conflict in relationships is often based in the ways we are different and have possibly misunderstood each other. When we feel safe to disagree and still be accepted (even when we are wrong and we have to admit it—or maybe *especially* when we are wrong) there is a level of respect that allows us to be ourselves.

When these four levels of connection have been achieved (*needs met, sameness, belonging,* and *significance*), Dr. Neufeld notes that children will begin to feel the emotions of connections—the "romance" of being loved and of loving another person. Around age four, children will talk about love—usually for their parents or siblings. They are following an instinct that pursues a deeper connection. Children who have been made to feel safe and significant in their home are now ready to "give away their heart"—***share their secrets*** and be known.[9] This level of self-disclosure—sharing of heart and soul, is the goal of any relationship—it is where we are most fully known and seen by another person who is important to us. This stage follows naturally when we have been accepted at the level of significance.

This is not something we "teach" to children with words. We model it with our own meaningful relationships, including those we have built with our children. But the instincts inside all of us are there to connect us in significant, life-giving ways. As Brene Brown says, the deepest need we have and the core of our DNA is that we are wired to connect with other humans. We are most satisfied by the relationships that have reached that stage where we trust someone enough to tell them our inner joys and struggles.[10]

These stages of connection build an ever-deepening sense of attachment inside of families, so Dr. Neufeld calls them "roots." Between adults, we follow the same pattern, but friendships are more likely to grow as we deliberately cultivate them. Between friends, I see the image as a ladder of connection, where we climb a bit higher in that friendship, toward the sharing of our inner hopes and dreams after we have established belonging and significance.

---

[9] *Neufeld, Neufeld Intensive 1, 2015.*

[10] *Brene Brown, Daring Greatly (New York: Penguin Random House, 2012).*

In my experience in travelling to the airport on public transport that winter morning, I climbed this ladder a few rungs—at least I started in that direction. The first young woman and I shared food, which drew us closer as we chatted about what we had in common. We had a glimpse of that sense of belonging between us by the end of the journey—but it usually takes months or years to set these rungs in place.

Generally the traditional cultures I've encountered don't look for truth in words, but rather in deeds. Instincts work to play out these stages of connection, but they are rarely talked about. Even conflicts have to be resolved by showing loyalty rather than by talking through the problems. Words can be empty and vain, and what you say sometimes doesn't mean you will follow through. Actions are where our values are revealed.

The differences can have a big impact if we are climbing a friendship ladder that combines cultures, and misunderstandings can threaten the friendship in the early stages. But if we can get past the stage of significance, there is a level of understanding that seems to overcome the differences and allow us to thrive in the friendship. It takes the commitment of time and effort—but then again, most great friendships require that from us.

TIPS, SUGGESTIONS AND QUESTIONS:

As you seek to form relationships across cultures, understanding that there is a natural hierarchy in the formation of relationships and trust can be a road map for you. Start by meeting the new friends' physical needs, usually through a gift of food or shelter. Take time to affirm the ways you share things in common, the values you are both aligned with, and the experiences that help you to understand each other. Allow that to grow into a sense of belonging and loyalty, letting your friend know that you will stand up for them and be on their side if there is a choice. And following that, don't be afraid to point out how significant the friendship is to you even if there are obvious differences.

Pay attention to the customs of the people you are befriending and ask about them in a curious and genuine way. Many cultures won't open gifts in front of you—you can ask, without judgment and maybe on the next visit, what is considered polite.

There may also be little sayings that surround customs of eating, offering hospitality, or giving gifts. These may differ even from one village to the next, so the details need to be learned from your new friends—you can't generalize. These little sayings are a big clue into the culture. Where I lived, people constantly said, "*Inistik bi hom*" with reference to my children—"Enjoy them." How lovely to be in a culture that reminds you every day to delight in your children!

If there is a misunderstanding created in your relationship, go back and affirm the things in common, but also speak about the ways that you value what is different and how it has enriched your life.

QUESTIONS FOR REFLECTION:

Can you see and trace the relationship ladder (needs met, sameness, belonging, significance, self-disclosure) in relationships in your family—your childhood or with your own children as they matured?

Can you identify a relationship in your life that draws you back by the comfort it has offered over the years? Is there a time that you can recall that sense of safety and comfort being built by physical needs being met? Can you trace the layers of relationship that are described here—needs met, sameness, belonging and significance?

~ 4 ~

When Mistakes Make Room for Grace

Grace means that all of your mistakes
now serve a purpose
instead of serving shame.
Randy Temple

Just as the human brain is wired to learn a language in the first few years of life, so it is also wired to form relationships with significant people in our lives. Understanding the progression from acquaintance to trusted friend can be helpful when cross-cultural friendships are in the formation stage.

Although we don't follow our instincts into relationships the same way that children do, these patterns are still within us as adults. The attention we give to our similarities is an important initial building block in most of our adult friendships. We tend to enjoy talking to people when we have something in common. Finding the ways we are alike opens up a whole new realm of discussion.

Last fall I was invited to a cross-cultural dinner hosted by the Turkish community where we live. The families giving this invitation wanted to build understanding and community in our city by offering a shared meal (of course). It was a cold night. My toes and fingers were starting to hurt as I sat outside at a makeshift table, eating delicious Turkish food cooked by a group of women who were still in the kitchen. But I knew they were honouring us with the food, and barging into the kitchen would have been too Canadian for me—and probably for them, since I don't speak Turkish.

When one of the cooks came to sit and chat, my heart warmed, and my cold hands and feet were less distracting. This woman, Zeynep, had four children, like me. She had lived in Canada for over a decade, just as I had lived in North Africa for over ten years. Her English was stilted and accented, and I sensed her discomfort at conversing with me in a language she found challenging.

I may have imagined it, but it seemed Zeynep was a bit guarded—waiting to see if I might judge her for not speaking better English. I identified strongly with the defensive stance of waiting to see if I was going to be accepted, flaws and all, or compared with someone and lambasted with criticism. As I drew out all the ways we were alike and commented on them, she relaxed and chatted happily with me. Relief swelled inside me at being the one conversing in my native language. I also felt my heart fill up with satisfaction at making her feel confident in the joy of a conversation—this is what we had both come for.

About fifteen minutes later, Zeynep's father came to join us. As he entered into the conversation, she became the translator for him. His English was virtually non-existent. We struggled to find our way into a conversation until I mentioned that I had a grandson. Out came his phone, and he proudly showed me all the photos of ten grandchildren in various locations across the world. The conversation between us flowed, sometimes too rapidly for his daughter, now completely unconcerned about her language level as she served as translator. His confident assumption that I would be interested in each picture was based in the discovery that I shared the grandparenting experience. How could I not want to hear about his grandchildren? And he was right—I did!

Finding ways that we are alike is a usual step in a relationship that is about to blossom. Once that stage has been established on solid footing, it is likely that we will grow into a sense that we belong together. When we acknowledge someone's importance with food, we give a message that we are delighted to meet them. That first invitation is like a seed planted, with the hope of germination at some point. The invitation of belonging is more like the coming of springtime blossoms—the assurance that sweet fruit is now on its way. But both of these promises have one thing in common: they take time.

If food is the first (and second and third) love language, and if it has that life-giving place in a traditional culture, this means it also holds a particular power to offend or hurt someone of that culture. I discovered just how much potential there was to harm a relationship with a wrong food choice when I was still quite new to North Africa. I learned this, of course, the hard way.

My children made friends with children from two families in the neighbourhood. I got to know one of the moms, Selma, and slowly she became my friend. She had four children who, together with another three children from the neighbourhood, adopted our living room as their communal play area. I loved this—it was a chance for my children to play and to learn the local dialect in safety. Playing on the street had proven quite hazardous for my oldest son, where he got bullied. Selma's children always spoke politely and there was no pushing or hitting when they came over.

In our large, unfurnished living room, scenes were re-enacted where the older kids were teachers and the younger ones were school kids. Games like Jenga and Go Fish became group favourites, and my kids learned to play a local favourite, *Shkulba*. My daughter learned to play the drums and dance to local rhythms—she was alarmingly good at belly dancing by the time she turned six. I had a great vantage point to learn cultural nuances.

The problem was, our budget was groaning under the demand for making extra food for seven extra children, often in our home for five or more hours at a time. Since I knew how important it was to make them feel welcome with food, I included them in our mealtimes. This was a real challenge since I never knew whether they would eat heartily or eat just a bite to be polite and then refuse the rest, which I threw away, being a germ-conscious Canadian. This was quite hard for me.

I decided to ask at another home where I had seen the children coming and going. As local people (and cultural experts, I assumed), what was their advice? Was I expected to feed these children? Was it rude to *not* feed them? Well, I failed to note the obvious, and I failed to ask the right questions!

First of all, the women I asked for guidance were not friends with the two mothers, though the little girls sometimes came to visit in their home. Secondly, they were both unmarried with no children of their own. They were polite-but-across-the-street neighbours, not friends.

The counsel I got was that it was just fine for me to **not** feed the seven children that had turned my front room into a full-scale daily play station, complete with party music and of course, belly dancing.

One day after the great fun of spending hours together, I decided to *not* invite the seven children for supper. They had been in my house for six hours, I had given them a suitable snack, and I really didn't want to throw away any supper that night. I told them in my Canadian way that it was time to go home. They filed out the front door silently with their chins hanging down to their chests, and I suspected I had erred.

I had forgotten to ask my third neighbours, the cultural informants, the right question—*HOW* should I ask the children to leave in an appropriate and polite way? In fact, it was not really the right question to ask—instead, I should have just observed how this would be indicated in a similar situation.

I had, in my ignorance, committed a major social blunder.

This was confirmed when I went to visit one of the moms a couple of days later. My friend Selma greeted me coldly at the door, refusing to bend toward me when I leaned in to kiss her cheeks. She sat on the edge of her chair like she was waiting for me to leave. She barely talked and certainly didn't ask about my family at home, a social obligation in any visit. She offered me no drink, something that was immediately offered normally, followed up with an offer of food a little later on.

I decided to be a dumb foreigner, acting as if I had not noticed. This was how I had learned to deal with other awkward situations when I was not sure if I was doing something wrong. This time I was quite clearly in the wrong, but I stoutly decided to test my technique in this awkward and chilly climate.

It sufficed.

After a few more stilted moments of one-sided conversation with my side being robust and cheery, some other guests arrived. Selma jumped up to greet them with gusto, welcoming them with all the warmth she had siphoned off of my greeting. She sat for about two minutes, chatting and asking about their family. Then she took off energetically down the hall to her kitchen, returning five minutes later with two plates heaped with a sandwich and some goodies. These were handed to the *other* guests, the *good* guests.

I was indeed *persona non grata.* Not even a chilly glass of water for me.

The new guests look confused, perplexed, and perhaps a little embarrassed as they tried to refuse the unexpected food. They were clearly not expecting a meal and kept glancing over to see how I was handling this clear violation of social propriety. I remained studiously stupid, oblivious to the insult. Everyone seemed to sigh a little in relief, and the visit went on.

The point of Selma's spear was a little lost on me. I was not unaware of her message, but my cultural background didn't contain the same weave of values that allowed this humiliation to stick to me. It would be akin to someone in Canada having a group of guests in and everyone raving about how out of date the colour pink is while the first guest to show up had arrived in a pink dress and sat through this discussion in silent shame—unless she didn't understand English. I pretended not to speak the language of food shame.

My visits with Selma continued for a few more weeks with this chilly atmosphere ruling her welcome. I fed her children the next time they came to visit and never asked them to leave again, though they were a little more discerning as well. This *faux pas* on my part eventually worked itself out when Selma had a heartfelt need and I was there with a generous answer to her pain. But in the meantime, I had learned a few valuable lessons!

Selma and I shared a few things in common, including the group of children who loved each other. We had started to build a solid sense of connection and belonging between our families. When I blundered and sent her children home, it was not the end of the friendship but rather an event that pushed us into the level of significance. My persistence in returning to her home communicated that Selma was important to me even after she had been rude and retaliatory using the local food culture to express her displeasure. In her eyes, I was the one who was rude and possibly punitive, by refusing to feed her children—so to her, my persistence in building relationship was a means of overcoming *my* shortcomings and bad behaviour.

I had previously built a strong relationship of belonging with Selma, and I relied on that to overcome the moment when I nearly fatally offended her. But what we did not yet have was a foundation of significance—she didn't see my friendship as valuable even though I was different. There would come a day when that would be a crucial turning point for us, but in the meantime I continued to wade into the stage of belonging and it worked. For the next few months there was a chill to her side of the friendship which I resolutely set out to influence with my sunshiny side.

Sometimes it is actually our mistakes that allow us to display our commitment to a friendship. We can't be daunted by the things we don't know and the mistakes we might make—we will almost certainly fail at some point. But if we believe there will be grace for those moments, they will become part of a bigger picture that is all the stronger for them. If we respect that our differences build the significance of the place we hold in a relationship, we will hold on to the times when we are misunderstood as part of a bigger picture. That bigger picture is a stronger relationship where mistakes, misunderstandings and even offenses build stronger foundations into the relationship.

Redemption is another word for the core message of the Gospel. If you don't have mistakes or flaws, you don't have room for redemption (not that any of us have that problem). Too many of us are hoping that we won't actually find ourselves in a mess that requires God's grace to cover and redeem us—but the message of hope is clear. Love covers a multitude of shortcomings, whether they are accidental or intentional, morally grave or completely inconsequential.

I became more aware of what the grace of God covers in my inadequacy. As I saw all that could be redeemed out of my failings, I began to see that the Gospel works mysteriously through the very hardest things in my life. I became less concerned about the mistakes that I *might* make and more focused on the love of God. His presence in my life means that grace covers my blunders.

TIPS, SUGGESTIONS AND QUESTIONS:

There are a few things to know about and avoid in this dance with the invitation to relationship, but if you are genuinely kind and caring, mixed with polite persistence, any missteps should work themselves out. If you show that you feel self-conscious or nervous about making a mistake, this might be taken as a sign of disinterest or rejection of the friendship.

People generally love to see pictures of family and tell you about their own family. Be ready with your phone to share, and show a generous interest in other people's family. Hearing their story of how they arrived in our country is an important way of sharing, even if the story is hard or sad.

Because hospitality is such an important "art" in the East, it is taken for granted that everyone knows how to be a confident, welcoming host. Above all, don't second guess yourself, and don't misinterpret someone else's facial expression (like I did in my first weeks) as a negative reaction!

As you look at relationships with someone from a new culture, it might help to consider that this is a new dance, and as with most dances we learn, there are times when we step on each other's toes.

QUESTIONS FOR REFLECTION:

How can you become better at observing the "dance" between people in their own culture? Are there events you can attend, or times you can sit and watch how they relate to each other—what can you learn from this?

How do you want to be able to evidence the gift of grace through any and all mistakes that you make? Is this important to you? Are you comfortable (yet) with the idea that God's light shines through us even or especially when our imperfections are seen by others?

~ 5 ~

Jonah's Journey Meets Mine

True prayer is asking God for what He wants.
William Barclay

It was our third springtime in North Africa, so I was getting used to the abrupt shift from cold to hot in March. By May it was full-on summer, which we decided only started when the thermometer registered over 40C (104F). I had coined a saying—

"Insanity is spending the winter waiting for summer to come—telling yourself the heat can't be as bad as this cold. And then spending the summer waiting for winter, telling yourself the cold can't be as bad as this heat"

It was hot. Scorching hot.

As I lay on the sofa in our living room with my face a few inches from a fan, I listened for the voices of my three children playing just beyond the window in our front yard. We had the misfortune of renting a house with a low fence and a gate that could be opened by someone on the street unless we chained it, which seemed a bit extreme when we were at home. Maybe those features, along with the surrounding rough neighbourhood, explained why it was available for rent. It was a spacious house, but the yard was small with faded, undulating tile.

Neighbourhood kids often played soccer in the empty lot across from our front gate. They seemed to enjoy asking for water from the garden hose when they had kicked the ball into our front yard. When they were thirsty, the ball came over the wall often, and they would ring the bell at our front gate insistently. I tried to discourage them from deliberately kicking it over the wall by walking to the door slowly. I wondered if they actually kicked the ball over to see if we were irritated by their antics. I would hand out glasses of water with a little bonus—a prayer for the recipient to seek the water of life, Jesus, one day. "This is my chance to bless them," I would tell myself. It kept me from resenting the frequent requests.

Almost.

My back was tight with pain as I lay on the sofa that day, hoping they wouldn't intrude with requests for water. My oldest son, playing in the front yard, could throw the ball back over the fence, so I had a good chance to take a break. I needed this rest before getting up to make supper, and I may have drifted into a short sleep. Suddenly the happy sound of my children laughing and boys playing soccer was replaced with intense snarling and the barking of a large German shepherd. It sounded like a full-on attack was imminent.

Behind the dog's angry snarls, I could hear my children screaming at the top of their lungs, but they were no longer under the window. I struggled off the sofa, unable to hurry due to my backache. I was seven months pregnant, and this pregnancy, combined with the heat, had taken its toll. On this day, just getting to the front door was a half-marathon.

As I peered out of the barred window in the middle of the front door, I jumped backward a step, wincing at the abrupt movement. There on the front porch facing me was a young man in his early twenties. Directly in front of me, backed up against the door, snapping and snarling at his owner, was the angry German shepherd. I had never seen this dog without a sturdy leather muzzle strapped securely over his mouth, but today he was loose on my front porch without it. And he was erupting with aggression.

I could see my children standing in the street, surrounded by a crowd of neighbourhood kids who were shouting at the young man. Their screams crescendoed above the din of barking and shouting.

I began to pray for my children to be safe—if the dog rushed out the gate onto the street, he might attack the smallest child out there—my little son, not yet three years old. I prayed for terror to leave them alone as this was clearly a traumatic situation. Then I prayed for the neighbour to manage his dog and regain control. Watchdogs were treated maliciously in order to breed a vicious response in them. I could see that the young man was himself in fear of the dog, now loose on the porch between me and my children.

Somehow my young neighbour got hold of the dog and put the leash and muzzle in place, and the two of them moved through my front gate where both sides hung wide open on the hinges. Someone had deliberately opened the gate and let the dog in. Was this done as a prank—to scare my children?

Possibly out of respect for my need to get to my children, the dog owner stopped at the gate and stood there as I passed. Maybe he wanted to say something to me. His German shepherd was still snarling inside his leather muzzle and tugging on the leash, but this was how I was used to seeing him. I told myself to stay calm and marched on out toward the kids. As I approached the gate, my little prayer—"This is my chance to bless"—flashed into my mind.

"I can't do that, Lord." I said this with the same purposefulness that I had for getting out to my children, who were now standing on the opposite side of the street, holding hands and sobbing.

"Love your enemies. Bless those who curse you." This thought flashed up into the conversation we were having—God and I. I had started the conversation by requesting His help with the dog—now I was getting God's end of the bargain—His request for me. Blessing your enemies is hardest in the middle of a battle. On this day, it proved to be too much of a request.

As I walked past the dog and owner standing tethered to each other just outside my gate, I muttered under my breath, "I will not curse you, I will not curse you." I lowered my eyes as I passed them, fearing I would say something scathing if I looked up.

"There. I didn't curse them," I stormed at God. "I couldn't bless him, but I didn't curse anyone." I thought God should be satisfied with this level of self-control given the circumstances.

I gathered my children first into a hug and then back into the house, locking the door behind us. I found something for us to do together—calming and restoring our sense of being safe together through this upheaval.

It took me weeks to reflect on all that had gone through my mind and indeed my spirit in those short minutes. I had wanted to curse the dog's owner and all the boys involved in letting the dog into our yard. My anger and resentment for a variety of earlier incidents had risen inside of me, exploding with frustration and unnerving me with its intensity. This was not the first animal the boys had opened the gate for—in the past year, sheep had been ushered in to graze on my struggling roses and verbena. It was, however, the last time they let an animal in—so maybe there was a sobering effect of this incident on everyone.

What had happened inside of me was not a feeling I wanted to face. I had wanted to say "DAMN YOU" as I passed the gate. A desire had risen up inside of me to see the young man suffer for his action—if indeed he had been the perpetrator—I didn't know for sure, but in the moment that had not mattered.

I was shocked by the strength of my toxic wish for revenge. And I struggled still to let the words of Scripture prevail inside of me —"Vengeance is mine." The idea that God would take care of justice, that I should focus on blessing an enemy was **not** something I was willing to entertain.

By definition, an enemy is someone you don't want to love. This command from Jesus, "Love your enemies, bless those who persecute you," is by nature challenging—on so many levels. On this day it was no longer just theoretical.

You have heard that it was said, "Love your neighbour and hate your enemy." But I tell you, love your enemies and pray for those who persecute you, so that you may be children of your Father in heaven. For he causes his sun to rise on the evil and the good, and sends rain on the righteous and the unrighteous. Matthew 5: 43-45 CSB

I knew that mercy didn't exist unless it existed for all people equally—the good, the bad, the really, really ugly. This day had been ugly. Inside me, its impact had been ugly.

For the first time in my life I understood the prophet Jonah and his reaction to the people of Nineveh. When God sent Jonah to share a message of repentance and salvation, he first of all didn't go. When Jonah finally got there, he refused to preach the message because the people didn't deserve to be saved—in Jonah's eyes anyway.

On this crazy hot day, I saw Jonah as someone who deserved my sympathy. It seemed as if maybe God was on the wrong side in the story of Nineveh—almost. I knew I was wrong to think this, but I struggled to move my own heart toward grace. The first step in that struggle was to own my emotion of retaliation.

Jonah's story rattled inside me for weeks—I didn't want to be the bad guy sitting under the shade of a vine God had provided for me. But I was. Every time I looked at my little garden, set in fading, uneven tiles, I was reminded of God's gift of that vine for Jonah to rest under…and the worm that came to eat it away. I saw my own nature as clearly as if a mirror had been held up for me to see myself in vicious, aggressive, snarling revenge. The message was unmistakable.

I could not pray for God's mercy and grace to come to this city, to bless these people, to break the hold of despair and darkness over them—I could not pray this from a pedestal where I looked down on the people I prayed for. I needed these gifts just as much as they did. I deserved condemnation as surely as they did. I was offered grace on exactly the same basis as it should be made known to them—God's goodness, not my own.

My self-righteousness stood staring back at me from the reflections of this day. I was not a faithful image of God's goodness so long as I lived, gave out water, befriended people, or shared my faith from the stance of superiority.

This changed how I prayed—which was crucial. It also changed how I viewed the categories of "us" and "them." I knew well what it felt like to be labelled "one of them"—an outsider. Some days I felt like my neighbours viewed me almost as if an extra-terrestrial being had moved in next door. People would peer over our fence and talk about us as they walked past our house, and I could understand enough to get the gist. We were bizarrely strange in our ways.

Humans naturally tend toward a vision of culture where we feel comfortable with people we would include in an "us" statement. And though we had talked about this in our home, some days it was a struggle to resist an "us versus them" division in this new country. When I started to view people from the local culture as "them," I knew I had slipped. I tried to watch out for that attitude.

What crept into my thinking with greater subtlety was the idea that I had the "right" way to God, and theirs was "wrong." Of course there were and are elements of their religion that I strongly disagreed with. But the elements of my own faith that needed to settle more deeply into my own soul included a deeper understanding of grace. This incident had forced me to see my own need for grace. When I have embraced my own need for grace, it is much easier to offer others the same generosity of spirit.

I am no more worthy of God's smile than anyone I meet, neighbour or stranger, wealthy or beggar. It's always tempting to approach people in need out of an inner belief that we have something of value to offer—it feels good to help another human. But over and over I find stories that tell me that most often the giver is blessed by the one they are trying to assist.

TIPS, SUGGESTIONS AND QUESTIONS:

In this story there are elements of culture that I didn't have to agree to or with. How dogs are treated, for example is much different in my own culture, and there were later times in my life when I influenced friends to treat their dogs differently. What other elements of the culture do you see in the story? Have you seen other things that might be cultural that you can disagree with honestly—just have a different opinion without having to argue the rights and wrongs of it?

One of the differences that we need to understand is that what we think of as "polite" is not considered necessary in another culture. Where we lived saying "please" or "thank you" is not necessary, but a failure to say "Good morning/afternoon" even to people in a shop you enter is exceptionally rude. These distinctions are arbitrary—there are other ways to show gratitude, but words are not involved. It is extremely important to realize that protocol (ways of being polite) can differ from place to place. If we don't recognize this, we easily misjudge people as lacking good manners, when in reality good manners are expressed very differently in their culture (and might be more valued by them than in our own culture).

In this chapter I talked about being the outsider, being labelled as "them." Have you experienced a time when you could easily see the division of "us and them"? How did it feel to be in one of those categories? It may not have even been cultural, it may have been in your school days, for example. How did it feel to be treated as an outsider?

Watching for differences and the categories of "us and them" really becomes harmful when we portray this with an attitude of exclusivity and superiority. It is impossible to ignore that there are differences between cultures—that in itself is not wrong. Respecting that there are differences we can learn from and admire, and learning to hold the ones we don't admire with an attitude of grace—these are elements of how the Gospel (grace and redemption) is integrated into even the smallest of our daily interactions.

QUESTIONS FOR REFLECTION:

Can you think of a time when you saw your own inner attitude as one that was not godly? What caused you to see this, and what did you do with that revelation?

How does humility combined with mercy move us toward embracing the foreigner we live near or who has come to live among "us"? Is your social network generally working to abolish the "us and them" mentality or are you (perhaps unwittingly) contributing toward keeping those barriers in place? What can you do to change this?

~ 6 ~

Only the Best

What do we live for,
if it not to make life
less difficult for each other?
George Eliot

After we had lived in our second country for about five years, a zoo opened along the highway an hour's drive from our home. This new destination for a family outing was a big deal. We valued our family day out, but it was hard to find a good destination. Quite often we'd spend the day somewhere and decide it wasn't worth a second visit—days out were a challenge. This new zoo, however, didn't disappoint any of us.

The animals were in free-range enclosures. It took a few hours to walk through the whole zoo, visiting each site and learning about the animals' habitats. Halfway through there was a restaurant with affordable prices and a view overlooking some low hills and a rolling valley beneath us. This was green only in the early spring, but we enjoyed the peace and quiet on the wide patio as a special treat—most restaurants were dingy and crowded.

After a couple of visits to the zoo, my husband befriended the young man who kept the camels. Samir saw our interest in animals and suggested we should come and meet his father who was a Bedouin shepherd.

The conversations in the camel pen resulted in a friendship with Samir's whole family. We could see the friendship was important to them. Their village was pleasant, his sisters were easy to be with, and best of all, they had a little old house with a round roof that served a dual purpose as a slide. When our six-year-old son fell head first off that roof, fracturing his arm but thankfully not breaking his neck, the whole family drove to our home to wish him well and deliver a bottle of fresh camel's milk—the best thing for mending bones.

Our son was less than enthusiastic about this gift. It was raw, unpasteurized milk, mild in flavour, and with a high fat content which tasted delicious in coffee. I had not had cream for coffee in a long, long time, so I justified my bones needed good milk too. It was a generous gift expressing Samir's family's devotion to our son's well-being since camel's milk is rare and expensive.

On some visits we stayed overnight in Samir's family home, mainly because their insistence felt like such a genuine invitation. The North African perception of time meant less than 24 hours spent in their home was an "incidental" visit. Only when we stayed overnight were we told that our visit really counted. The siblings' mother had died, and the daughters responded to us with a bubbly joy that was hard to resist. Some of our children found it hard to stay in homes where the privacy of the only toilet was a flimsy striped curtain that flapped with any breeze. The "toilet" found inside was a hole constructed in such a way that it required a special talent to keep your feet clean and dry when you used it.

On one of our visits, Samir's family proudly showed us through the brand new rooms prepared for the next brother to get married. These rooms even had a privacy-rich bathroom—with a door and a lock. The tiles in all these rooms were bright and shiny and recently cleaned, which might have been a clue to us, but we missed it. The family told us that no one could live in this wing of the household until the bride arrived, out of honour for her. Even so, we were taken there after nightfall along with the mattresses we had been sitting on at supper time. A sister traipsed along behind us carrying a stack of warm blankets. Once those mattresses and blankets were lined up on the clean new floor, we were set for the night.

Only the best for guests.

We felt conflicted about taking these rooms—it was as if we were stealing from the honour that had been reserved for the bride. This was to be her new home—clean, unused, unsullied in any way.

But the family clearly felt that this honour should be ours. They would not be truly generous hosts if we were not offered the very best.

I struggled with this part of the culture every time local friends came and stayed in our home. I felt guilty not only that I didn't offer my bedroom with the best bed in the house, but beyond that—I didn't even *want* to offer it to them.

One Christmas, when our South African friends joined us for several days, I finally got this concept. We had two families coming, which filled our house and took up all the beds. Then more friends called, and these additional, unexpected guests meant we had to get creative with sleeping options.

I could give someone the floor to sleep on, or I could give the South Africans our bed. These friends had almost become parents to us—they had given us a "sheltered place" in their hearts, and mentored us in parenting our young teen children. It was unthinkable to have them sleep on the floor. I felt honoured to offer them a good sleep under my warm duvet. It was unusual for me to feel this way, as my bedroom was a place of sanctuary when I needed a place of retreat—it was my sanity keeper.

But giving your best room—the best bed—is the cultural norm in the Middle East and North Africa. There is honour in serving the best you have, and that virtue is what motivates the gift. Even the clothing you wear to visit someone is seen as an indicator of how much you honour them. If you wear old, casual clothing on a visit to someone's home, this can be an indicator that you don't esteem them very highly. It is always better to be overdressed than underdressed in North African culture. If you are the only one who has your best dress on, there is no need for embarrassment. It is seen as a sign of respect and honour.

This giving of the best to others is a mentality that seems to be the opposite of what we have in our individualistic and self-serving culture. We work hard and then save the best for ourselves, feeling we have earned this privilege and deserve to treat ourselves well. We deem it a cruel sacrifice should we feel obligated to give the coveted "best" away.

Generosity is at the heart of hospitality. But many traditional cultures take this benevolence to a level we find hard to imagine. Even after years in North Africa, I often felt I was only beginning to embrace this value that I could see had potential to change me for the better.

A few years after the camel's milk was delivered to our home, Samir announced near Christmas time that his family would be coming to join us for our Christmas feast. The word "feast" doubles as a meal and a holiday. Sure enough, two farm trucks arrived, bringing all ten of the family. I had served a turkey dinner the night before, anticipating that I should serve Samir's family local cuisine on this visit. But they insisted that they had come all this way in order to try our food, share our feast.

I had plenty of turkey dinner leftovers—anticipating that we would enjoy that meal again in a day or two. The sisters' enthusiasm for trying our feast food convinced me that they might enjoy it. Common sense screamed the opposite, but given their efforts to convince me, it would have been rude to refuse. I piled the plates high with couscous on one side and turkey, potatoes, and stuffing on the other. Generosity with food expresses how much you value your guests, whether they like the food and devour it—or not. The obligation, or honour, is all on the side of the host—who offers his or her best.

An hour after I'd loaded up the plates, I was scraping everything but the meat from our turkey feast into the garbage. Our foreign food tasted pasty and bland—in a word, disgusting. Their palates were built for fiery fuel. The turkey went into the soup pot, but the rest went into the garbage—too much for our pets to consume.

As I stood scraping plate after plate into the black bag, I reflected on my own attitude with triumph. *I had finally arrived!* I was internally aware that it didn't matter a whit that they didn't like my cooking, and I was pleased with myself that I had honoured them by piling their plates high with our very best. I felt no resentment toward them for wasting our resources. They indeed had not been wasted. I had used our treasured leftovers for the best of purposes, to honour our guests—*even if they didn't eat them, I had given them honour.* My pleasure gave me a sense of inner triumph. I felt satisfied.

It had taken me about seven years to let the culture change me this much, but I was surrendering to the values I loved best about this community. People over things, every day of the week.

It is a universal reality that a feast marked by generous portions of food is central to most family reunions and celebrations. These feasts mark the passage of years in all cultures and religions. Children worldwide look forward to special holidays with the thrill of anticipation, and then those occasions draw us like magnets throughout our adult years, back to the memories that give us comfort and joy. Or, in some cases these memories are frail or absent and we are reminded of the abyss of unrequited love and unfulfilled expectation that marked our childhood.

In those rituals of feast and celebration, the true nature of that family is likely to be revealed....are there joyful moments when we are bound together by laughter and joy? Are the rituals of belonging strong and deep, calling us back to our family to enjoy days of celebration? Christmas and Easter for most Westerners, the two Eids for Muslims, for Sikhs, Diwali and Holi—but worldwide, these rituals of food and celebration glue us together with culture and tradition.

If we dig deep into our intentions, a generous feast that is joyful and gives nourishment to both body and soul is what we aim for with our Christmas celebrations and family dinners. But the protocol in our culture is not as clearly laid out as it is in most traditional cultures.

One of the best lessons I learned from living abroad was that generosity reflects God's own character. As I encountered this, I began to realize that the essence of redemption and grace is the audaciously generous offer of God himself to become human and live and die as one of us. Yet still He is God.

We talk about a God who is rich in mercy, grace, and love, but we often act as if we are agents of a stingy, judgmental, self-righteous deity. The story of the Prodigal Son is ironically named for the son who was "recklessly lavish." In the story the son is lavish in spending his inheritance without regard for anything but his own pleasure. The irony of the story is that despite this obvious failing, there is another character who is recklessly lavish—the Father. He too, spends far too much, but in his case, there is a display of grace and kindness that cannot be faulted. When his older son questions the Father, the answer is yet another display of kindness and generosity.

God is the original host to humans, the One who gives us only His best. For me, the best line in this parable story, often lost in the dialogue, is the response the father gives to the older brother. When this son bitterly demands an answer as to why the father is being so generous with the errant, disgraceful younger son, the reply is astonishing: "My son, everything I have is yours." The bounty of the father's heart extends even in the face of a demand that is brimming with anger and resentment.

In Psalm 37 there is a long comparison of the characteristics of the wicked and the righteous. The Psalmist references the quality of generosity as a feature of godliness.

I have been young and now I am old,
yet I have not seen the righteous abandoned
or his children begging for bread.
He is always generous, always lending,
and his children are a blessing. Psalm 36:25, 26 CSB

In the Muslim faith that surrounded us in North Africa, there was an overt acknowledgement that generosity indicated godliness. When my neighbours saw my husband giving rides to people in our van or helping the poor, they commented to me that I was married to a godly man. Not just a good man (which he is), but a *godly man.*

Inviting someone into your own home, giving them the best you can afford, or the best you can bake, served on the best dishes you own—this is an honour to yourself and to the guests. It is an act that emulates the generosity of God, and it honours the gift of His own unrivalled best—His Son.

TIPS, SUGGESTIONS AND QUESTIONS:

Most Middle Eastern homes have a room that is reserved for guests. It is always kept in perfect condition, ready for guests. The furniture may be elaborate and even flashy or ornate while the rest of the house might be quite plain. This room is kept this way as an honour to guests. A guest would not be expected to come into the kitchen and "make themselves at home"—at least not until a friendship was established. This value of showing honour is truly a key thing to understand about culture.

In this chapter I suggest that giving has an element of honour to it—though it doesn't always feel that way in our culture. Have you met someone who seems to hold this value?

This gift of your best will undoubtedly impact any friendship, but the symbolism of this type of giving has power to transform any relationship you are building with someone from a traditional culture. You may not have enough money to go out and buy extravagant gifts, so it has to be about something other than money—if you think about this for a while, you will probably realize that there is something in your life that represents giving the "best" that has nothing to do with money. One of the ways this is expressed in North Africa is in how you are dressed for a visit—dressing up means you are honouring your guests.

When we lived in North Africa we noticed that whenever someone travelled they would come back with a gift for all their friends. It might be small if you were not close friends, but this gift meant something. It said, "I thought of you while I was away." It was an important expression of belonging and connectedness.

In our culture, offering "gently used" items between friends is usually acceptable. In some cultures this is considered an insult—giving something used to another person denotes that we consider them lower in status which would be insulting if the recipient thought they were a friend of equal stature. Be sure to find out if there is such a sense in the culture of your friends from other backgrounds so you don't make any offensive gestures, and never assume "beggars can't be choosers"—this attitude toward refugees and immigrants can easily lead to misunderstandings and offense.

If you have a friend from another culture, ask them what gifts mean—when they would give them or how, and what it would express. If you don't have such a friend, try either giving something to someone you might come across at work or if you have a child, another parent. See what happens... Or try this with a Western friend and just explore how it might change the nuances of that relationship.

QUESTIONS FOR REFLECTION:

Inviting someone home with you might make you feel quite vulnerable—have you ever stopped to ask yourself why you feel "unsafe"? (If you don't know why it feels so difficult, it may be worth discussing honestly with a friend.) It isn't easy to have people into your home if you have a hidden expectation of being judged or misunderstood—but it is better to face that and work with it, than to have it eat away at your confidence for years, unresolved. Sometimes we need to talk to ourselves about our unspoken expectations of criticism and make a decision to move beyond that. Sometimes it is just a case of identifying what kind of character we choose to value in ourselves and acting on that.

What kind of value do you put on generosity, and what kind of value do you want to put on it as a friend? If you have fears that are holding you back, identify them and talk about them with someone and make a plan that will push you one step toward overcoming them.

***Maria, who is from the Philippines**, lived in Afghanistan for six years. Here are some of her observations on living cross culturally:*

Filipinos put great value on hospitality. You may come to our house anytime and dine with us even if we are not expecting you at that time. We will go out of our way to prepare extra food so we can share a meal together. We love to hang out and eat. That is why it's shameful to offer nothing to eat or a place to sleep when someone pays us a visit. We give our best effort to make our guests feel special - best food, best clothes, even the best place in the house!

However, I discovered that the Afghans' hospitality is even more impressive than us Filipinos. An average Filipino family may offer two to three dishes but the Afghans would fill the long table with a variety of food. As a Filipino who finds being hospitable very precious, it was not difficult to spend hours of eating, drinking tea, and chatting with our Afghan friends.

I believe that in our ministry, our people live, behave, and work within an honour and shame culture and societies that cherish the extended family. As the Bible teaches us to be hospitable, the more we need to be hospitable to our people group. May we grow in deeper understanding of the people we are reaching and be able to demonstrate love in ways that identify with them so they would desire to know Jesu and to love Him and obey Him in their lives.

~ 7 ~

Time^2

Do the best you can
until you know better.
Then when you know better,
do better.
Maya Angelou

Time is money…and thus efficiency and progress should serve a specific purpose in how we use our time. If we are part of the West, this is the value we use to map our days. We plan and manage our time with a great deal of thought, giving it a special name: "time management skills." Since we only have 24 hours in any given day, we make the most of our time, because it will never be back. We live with the awareness that this is a one-shot deal!

No wonder we are dying, literally, of stress-induced diseases.

But are we willing to listen to the voice of change? Do we have room for another paradigm? Eastern and traditional cultures look at time completely differently—and we often criticize them for their differing values in how time is spent or measured. Efficiency is rarely the yardstick.

The culture of North Africa challenged so much in my life. In the area of time values, I had a lot to learn, and lucky for me—nowhere to go. Learning was becoming my unloved middle name.

In the early months of our time in North Africa, I found myself sitting in numerous gatherings where I felt lucky if I could come home with three new words that I could pronounce well enough for my husband to tell me the meanings. It was surely the slowest way to learn a language, but sitting for hours in a room full of women chatting with each other was a complete waste of time (to my way of thinking) unless I could accomplish something, even just three words.

Eventually I learned enough local dialect to carry on a simple conversation, and I would practice language with anyone who was patient enough to talk to me. Thus I began to feel these visits, which often lasted for five or six hours, had a little bit of purpose or meaning. At the two hour mark, I often felt like I had reached my limit—but that was considered a short visit in a culture where if you were a *real friend* you would come and stay for days, not hours!

I was completely unaware of the value of my silent presence in someone's home. The idea of honour—the honour of giving my time to someone by participating in a simple gathering—was lost on me. The sheer volume of time that was given to sitting in order to show a host that you were committed to the relationship felt burdensome and sometimes I even resented the demands of the culture.

My children knew how to do this—sit with other children, pouring sand in and out of containers—suspended in the moment. It is a skill that comes naturally to children, and they seem to be able to rest from any stress in those suspended moments of play. It is one of the most useful places for them to learn new things.[11] I could watch my daughter doing this with her friend in our garden, and I knew she was powering through learning this new language. But I failed to recognize that I had the capacity to enter into this place of being fully present to the moment I was in. I might have learned faster if I had noticed this.

I was from a more educated background, and the value of words and perceptions shared with others was a considerable part of my purpose in life. If I could not share my ideas, how could I participate meaningfully in community? And although that piece of the puzzle might be essential, rarely does it stand alone in a traditional culture. Over the course of many years and through a variety of events, this different view on how we spend time together would start to make more sense to me. But some of those learning occasions came because we were a part of the most painful events life would bring to those we loved.

We arrived at Leila's house on a Sunday morning, thinking we were here to offer our support to a grieving widow who had given birth to a fourth child just a few months after the traumatic death of her husband.

---

[11] *Deborah MacNamara, Rest, Play, Grow (Vancouver: Aona Books, 2016).*

The birth had been complicated, resulting in a C-section, and the baby had been transported to a specialized hospital an hour away. Leila was sent home to recover, without even seeing her newborn son.

My husband had gone out of his way to find the attending doctor, but the circumstances of the birth were vague, and frankly, quite suspicious. We approached the house with trepidation that quickly turned to heartache as we entered the cement courtyard. The greeting we were offered was the one uttered whenever there has been a death. Three days after the birth, Leila's baby had died—far from her in a teaching hospital, un-held and un-named. She had not even seen his face.

My husband sat down with the men in the courtyard while I went in to an unpainted living room, cold with the chill of winter and grief. There I knew I would sit in silence with the women—neighbours and relatives of all ages. Leila lay at one end of the room on a mattress, covered in blankets, facing the wall and moaning from time to time. I leaned in to kiss her face with the local greeting. I held her as close as possible against my chest for a few seconds.

The visiting women sat on sponge mattresses that lined the unfinished cement walls, serving as beds at night and couches during the daylight hours. There was no dialogue as a group—mostly we sat in a respectful silence. This was interspersed with a low hum of private conversation every now and then. It would have been unthinkable for these women to leave Leila alone on a day like this—being alone is rarely considered a good thing in traditional cultures. To allow someone who is ill or in grief to suffer without company is not a sign of respect, as we often see it in the West. It would have been considered abandonment to leave Leila alone. Even making a short visit on a day like this would be taken as disregard for the losses she had endured—first her husband and now her son.

From time to time another groan escaped from the pile of blankets that buried Leila and her grief. The groans came like waves, sometimes softly, sometimes filling the room with her sorrow. One or two of the older women would shout platitudes at Leila whenever she groaned, though I doubted that she was able to take in anything she heard.

After a while I noticed that the groans seemed to indicate that she was enduring significant physical pain. I asked the women what kind of medicine she had brought home. None, they answered. She was recovering from a C-section in the public hospital, where I knew they didn't take much time to put the stitches close enough together for optimal healing. And she had been given no pain meds.

I sent my husband home to get her the pain medication we had on hand. When he arrived, I assisted her in taking some, and the older women had a moment of recognition that perhaps I could help with another dilemma. Leila had been told to pump off her milk in order to prevent an infection. Did I have a pump? Did I know how to do this?

I no longer owned a pump, but I was familiar with the idea, which was clearly part of their concern. They had never even heard of this. Once again my husband went out, this time to find a pharmacy and purchase a pump, and I was commissioned to attend to this problem.

With an unfamiliar pump, in front of her guests, I crouched down over her prostrate body and did my best to relieve her of the swelling in her breasts. As I did so I prayed quietly, under my breath. The rest of the women sat watching, some from across the room, others from a few feet away. I tried to give some other comfort to Leila, touching her shoulder gently. I knew that anything I might do or say was unlikely to reach into her abyss. She lay moaning and it seemed to me, teetering on the cliff edge of a deep depression. Death beckons our souls to despair with more power than any other universal force.

I returned to my spot and sat for a little longer, and with the sun navigating its way into evening, one of the old women turned to me and invited my advice. Each time Leila groaned deeply, often entwined with a desolate wail, one or two of the women would bellow out their encouragement loud enough to drown out her groans. "Forget about this one, you have three other children to care for. Don't think about this one. God knows what He is doing—He took this one to Himself."

I had found this method of encouragement hard to endure throughout the afternoon, but I recognized it was not my place to dispute it.

Now, having spent the day, and having brought medications and taken care of Leila's milk, I had shown my respect and earned a place in the room. More importantly, by sitting silently in their company, observing this loss with them, enduring the sorrow alongside Leila—I had earned the right to be one of them.

So on this last bout of wailing and grief, one wizened old lady told Leila to forget this child then turned to me and said, "You tell her. Tell her to forget this child." I was now an expert, and the wrinkled auntie assumed I would be on her side.

"No," I said slowly, inserting a pause to breathe a prayer for wisdom between my words. "All children are a gift from the Lord. Each one is a treasure. No mother ever forgets any of her children. I cannot tell her that."

My language skills kept my sentences short and clear, but I don't think that is why no one chose to contradict me. They had spent the day speaking the opposite message, but now they were silent. The older women looked at each other and started to nod. "She speaks truth," they added, looking at the younger women.

Had I not spent time in their presence, a community of women woven together by their concern for a grieving widow and mom, I would never have been asked to speak. And my words would have been empty and unaccepted.

There were many other occasions when I was not offered a chance to speak, and no words would have sufficed as a message. My presence *was* the communication—just by being in the room or courtyard, I shared the communal voice that said, "You and your life matter." This unembellished message was the one we complicate so much with our Western conversations. In silence it is kept intelligible.

Without the gift of presence, anything I wanted to say would have been lost. At times my thoughts went unshared because no one asked and I recognized that without the invitation I would sound brash. Most often it was my presence that spoke, eloquently translated without my foreign, stumbling accent.

When Leila's brother got married a few months after their mom's death (that same year), some of the family were outraged that he didn't wait the full year as custom dictated. Tragedy had accumulated around this family and frayed their kindness toward each other. These family members boycotted the wedding in indignation. The oldest brother had decided the wedding should go ahead despite the circumstances, though normally a wedding within a year of a family death was forbidden. It was a fractious event.

The night of the wedding, I sat in the crowd outside the bride's home into the early hours of the next day—swatting mosquitoes and wishing to go home. The music blared, but few people danced; it was just too hot. As I sat thinking about my quiet, cool home, it dawned on me: nothing I could say about this wedding would be more articulate than my presence. By being here when the groom's own sisters had refused to come, I was declaring a blessing on the marriage, and I was honouring a bride as she deserved to be honoured. There were not enough words in the language for this message. Silence and presence spoke well enough.

We tend to know, in the West, that sitting together in grief is appropriate, but we often feel uncomfortable with the silence. We find it hard to sustain a relationship where words are unnecessary. Our instincts tell us that our time honours the family when someone's life has reached its end—but we are still not able to embrace that time itself is the gift.

In traditional cultures, time is a precious gift at weddings, school events, and social engagements of every kind. When you go to a school play, you might find yourself sitting through two hours of final preparations before the event actually starts. There may be music and a drink offered, but the waiting audience sits and chats as if—where else would I rather be? I'm here for the duration, and I can wait here as happily as I could sit at home watching TV—in fact, what a superb time we are having enjoying each other!

Time is considered one of the most precious gifts you can give—once you have given it away, it can never be recovered. And in many ways, it cannot be repaid. There will come a day when the honour is returned, but time is something we only get to spend once.

Generosity of time, coupled with leniency with the "results," is another of the ways God's character is displayed in all parts of the Bible. "Slow to anger" is just one of the phrases that reminds us that the Gospel comes with a different time feature than we tend to see in our culture. We look for an immediate response. Sometimes what is needed is the "gardener's" perspective—the idea that all good fruit comes from trees that are carefully tended over years in healthy conditions.

Time is not money in the East, and if it were, it would be used to buy or invest in community. And that is exactly how resources, both time and money, are best spent. I am grateful for the years I spent in a culture that taught me this lesson that defies lectures, textbooks and degrees of education.

TIPS, SUGGESTIONS AND QUESTIONS:

If you have a friend from another culture, make the effort to give them the gift of your time. Put aside all other thoughts and efforts and take a day to spend just focusing on being together—ask what they would do on a day together in their home in the city they came from. Try to match some of these activities and observe how they are performed—is a long walk taken at a leisurely pace that makes it longer? Is a meal prepared without any concern that it is taking all afternoon? Enter into her time pace and watch and see how that affects your relationship.

Try to get inside of some social situations where your friend interacts with people from her own culture. Can you observe anything that makes you think about this sense of time being suspended and the participants being at rest from the stress of needing to accomplish something?

If you sense it is a good time, open a discussion about how our culture views time, asking them to tell you about what we look like to other cultures. To get to this place in a relationship, where someone is able to articulate some of the things we do that just don't make sense, is sometimes a challenge. Don't be surprised if they don't feel too comfortable answering about this, but if you can get there, it is an amazing gift to start to see some of the ways we look "different" to people from other countries or cultures.

If you know someone is experiencing a loss, do not assume they want to be alone. Sitting in silence with them may be the best gift you can give.

Giving time to people's children is another great way to learn to be present. It also sends a strong message that you care for them—parents instinctively know that when someone cares about their children and spends time loving them, they are trustworthy people.

QUESTIONS FOR REFLECTION:

How much time do you spend on people and how much on efficiency? Do you agree that time has a value? Do you work with or know anyone from another culture? If you were to observe and then start a dialogue with them about how time is viewed differently in different cultures, how do you think they would respond?

From Elie Jo in North Africa:

Treating a friend like they are family—and having them treat you as family is truly important. It may not look the way you expect, as I found out:

When your friends start to treat you as family this is honouring! But that doesn't mean it is easy. I discovered this when I went to the wedding of some relatives of the family I was becoming part of. I was the only one there with a car…they asked me to run one errand after another and I did not feel gracious about it at all—I felt taken advantage of! I wondered and grumbled (thankfully inwardly-at least as far as I remember). We were at the wedding until 7am and then I drove everyone home and finally went to bed. *One **stinking hour la**ter* (!) they woke me up again to drive the wedding coordinator lady home…I was NOT HAPPY! But driving her back I had an epiphany.

If I was going to say we are family….then I needed to start acting like it! The one family member with a car is often asked to do all that…so they were just treating me like family, honouring me, which is what I always said I wanted. I SHUT UP!

Elie Jo Shaw

~ 8 ~

Open Homes—Open Hearts

Love like there is no tomorrow.
and if tomorrow comes, love again.
Max Lucado

In some cultures, homes are very private places and guests are rarely invited in. "Your home is your castle" is a strong mentality of protectionism, keeping people out. In other cultures, sometimes determined by climate and location, homes actually lack privacy. They may be built with a wide-open "view." Either way, when you are invited into someone's home, it is a gesture of trust and an opportunity to take a friendship to a deeper level.

The idea that there are still homes in the world where you can walk straight through someone's space unhindered by doors or walls is pretty far from where any of us live. But they still existed when I was a child—I know because I've been there.

My dad was a pilot flying into jungle airstrips, delivering food, mail, and medicine to Christian workers who lived in settlements alongside a native tribe. These families were committed to living in a community that was isolated by culture and language, often under threat of contracting disease from a local work crew clearing the jungle for agriculture. My dad sometimes took me along when he visited the "*Yuqui*" tribal group.

The workers there, Ted and Janet, lived in a little house Ted had built on stilts about two feet off the ground. Their house, while minuscule, had all the familiar spaces of a Western house—a kitchen, common room, and two tiny bedrooms. Ted was clearly a gifted builder. The *Yuqui* people lived in shelters that were nothing more than a simple thatched roof—no walls or windows or rooms, but still a home for cooking, living, and sleeping together.

We flew into the *Yuqui* jungle clearing one day with a guest, Dave, who was visiting us from our home city in Canada. Dave was physically disabled, so my dad took extra time to brief him about what to expect. The local people had no qualms about inspecting anyone's body for anomalies, and they would surely be intrigued by Dave, who was about the same size as I was—then ten years old. The three of us flew over miles of jungle in the peaceful hum of the tiny Cessna airplane before landing in the jungle to deliver mail and necessities.

As it happened, the *Yuquis* decided to abstain from this personal inspection on this day. I had taken a special precaution to wear clothing that would make it hard to "inspect" my body. It was a one piece "jump suit" with a long zipper up the front. I found out how unhelpful this was when I had to use the outhouse facilities before we left!

I was intensely relieved that we weren't inspected as we walked from the airstrip to Janet and Ted's little house to eat lunch with them. You can imagine that for these Americans living in a jungle village, a lunch with someone bringing city goods was a welcome treat. I was amazed at what Janet had cooked up in her basic kitchen. She was a true home-maker, with pretty tea towels hanging as curtains on her shelves in the tiny galley.

We sat down to lunch in Ted and Janet's main living space that had a window on every wall to catch any whiff of a breeze. The chatter of the local people made me a little uncomfortable. There, with their noses pressed against the screen windows on either side of us, was a robust and cheerful crowd of observers. In a language we could not understand, they were openly chatting about our every move. Ted was happy to translate at least part of what was being shared among them.

The social norms that would have tempered this kind of interest in the cultures I was familiar with were conspicuously absent. Raw curiosity etched itself on each of their faces. How many times had they seen Janet and Ted eat at this table? They must have known what to expect, but we were three extra guests, and which of us were the adults? It must have been like having a free ticket to the latest thriller at the Cineplex.

Years later I would recall our visit to this group of indigenous people and tell my children stories from our family adventures. Their school curriculum required them to write about Amazon jungles being repurposed as farmland, so we wrote to my dad and got a few more details about Ted and Janet's work. In this correspondence, one of the phrases my dad shared had an immediate and lasting impact on me.

"When you go into a situation like this (as Janet and Ted did), it takes about 10 years just to begin to understand the culture," he wrote.

I had been living in North Africa for 8 years when he wrote this, and I recognized the truth in what he was saying. It wasn't just in a jungle settlement with a completely different set of social norms that this was true. It was that culture is so deep and complex that we cannot say we have fully understood a new one until we have invested considerable time in becoming part of the community we are in.

When we encounter immigrants and refugees who have come to settle in our Western country, it would be remiss of us to think that they will understand our culture quickly or without an invitation to share our lives. We certainly don't live with open screen windows where they can stand and observe our mysteriously different ways of doing things! They have to learn from a distance that is often too great for them to see what we value and how we relate to each other in our closest relationships of family.

It takes courage and humility to invite someone home for a meal—and it is a rare gift. Our family has heard from a number of foreigners living in our Canadian city that they have received vague invitations, "We'll have to have you over sometime," or "Let's have coffee sometime." These invitations rarely materialize, much to the surprise and disappointment of the recipients. In other cultures, you usually don't talk about inviting someone to your house until you are setting a date and time, and it is considered duplicitous to talk about such an invitation but not follow through with it.

I don't think anyone in my home culture is deliberately misleading in making the gesture. But I do think we get cold feet when we consider more deeply or seriously what it means to have a foreigner over. We know we might make mistakes, serve food that is unappetizing, or fail to show hospitality at the level that honours our guests. Probably some of what I have written in previous chapters has made you even more aware of the pitfalls of these unknowns.

But the invitation to "come home with me" is one of the most compelling forms of friendship. We do it easily as children if we know that someone will take care of the details. We also do it confidently as children if we instinctively know our home is a safe place.

This is exactly what an invitation to a newcomer—an immigrant or refugee—represents. It is an invitation into the very safest place in our culture, a home. It is an offer of provision and protection in the most sacred space a family can have—a place of shelter and rest. When we invite someone home, we invite them into a gift that is much more than it seems to those of us with "new" cultures, Westerners.

The term "breaking bread" has several connotations, dating back to the beginning of time. Offering bread to a traveller still has a strong symbolic message of the gift of life to desert cultures. Traditionally, sharing a meal is a point in time when you would no longer wish harm on someone—it is a statement that you are giving the gift of friendship and of peace.

If you have met a foreigner and begun a friendship with them, by all means make the effort to invite them to your home. If it seems daunting to plan a menu and exhausting to do all the work to prepare a meal that is up to the standard of hospitality they have already offered to you, consider getting some help. Find someone you admire (from any culture) for their gift of hospitality and ask them how to make a meal that is not beyond your resources of time, energy, and money. Treating someone as an expert is an honour in any culture, so they might be delighted to assist you. If you need to buy most of your food in a deli or prepared for you, there are plenty of great services that offer delicious food.

Above all, don't portray discomfort at being the host. If you are nervous, your insecurity can easily be misinterpreted as something less flattering—most commonly it can be re-interpreted to mean, "You're not wanted here." Of course, you are hoping to express the opposite message.

The key to hospitality is to recognize that your role as host is to "rule with benevolence" in a way that is devoted to meeting your guests' needs. You are the decision maker, so make the decisions with confidence. When people see that someone is watching out for them, protecting them, and providing for their needs, this is an invitation to rest in their host's care. And this gift, of inviting someone in and providing rest for their souls, is one of the most precious gifts you can give.

Without this invitation to view how life takes place inside of a home, newcomers can get into a habit of meeting with others from their "home" country. They won't learn the culture of this new country unless someone "here" welcomes them into the inside, the family view. They don't have the option to stand at the screen windows and satisfy their curiosity from handy front-row seats! Even if they did, they probably wouldn't be comfortable with that, since it isn't a cultural norm in most of the world. So that leaves them with television, and the culture seen there is not what most of us want representing us!

There is the added tension that for most refugees and immigrants, their children will attend a local school and begin to learn basics about the culture there. When parents are unaware of some of those changes and adaptations, it is typical that a dissonance starts to divide their families. Sometimes these tensions even result in a complete family breakdown, which is heartbreaking for parents who wanted to give their children a better life in this new country.

Your invitation to a newly landed family to participate as guests in your home can be a gift to these parents and a lifesaver for their family relationships. You can make the offer to explain local culture if they have any questions. If you ask some non-threatening open questions about the culture they come from, this may pave the way to some helpful conversations. It may take a while for the trust to grow to this level, but your willingness to give your time and effort will not go unrewarded.

In this journey, it is likely that your own family will gain at least as much as you give. It's another spiritual principle that repeats itself over and over in our lives—when you set out to be a blessing, you will more than likely receive an even greater blessing.

As for the Gospel, the invitation into a family, the Father's family, is at the very core of who we are and who we are becoming. The invitation into our home expresses God's desire to know each one of our new friends as His son or daughter.

TIPS, SUGGESTIONS AND QUESTIONS:

As you engage with other people from other cultures, take time to observe how different families function, and how roles might be different in other countries. In particular, take a look at age—do older people have a different status or role in families than what you are used to?

If you have some errands to run, or somewhere to go, invite your new friends to go with you so they get a chance to see how you do things. Even learning how to get a shopping cart and go through a till can be daunting for someone who has never done this, and it can be just a fun excursion if they already know—make it a time for laughter. There is no glue like laughter for pulling a friendship tighter together! Offer to go on errands with your friends. I went to court with some new Canadians four or five times—it was daunting for me, even though I was just there to observe. I can't imagine how hard it was for them, or how much harder it would have been had I not offered my presence.

If you have children, talk with them about how it feels to have a family that surrounds you. Take time to observe if you have built a strong relational "ladder" in your own home, and ask your children to interact with how you could do that well (if they are old enough). Out of this discussion (which would be an important foundation) ask your children if they are willing to create a place of "family" for someone from another country who is new to your city—discuss how you could provide a feeling of being "at home" if you invited the family to participate in one of your "feasts."

QUESTIONS FOR REFLECTION:

Have you ever had someone that you invited into your family to participate as if they were one of you? Or have you ever been invited into a home where you felt you were almost "one of the family"? Have you ever stopped to consider how much this reflects on your faith in Christ? Have you ever stopped to ponder the words of Paul when he talks (in more than one place) of how we are adopted as sons (and daughters) of God?

~ 9 ~

When We Become Friends

When we seek to discover
the best in others,
we somehow bring out
the best in ourselves.
William Arthur Ward

Sometimes the biggest obstacle to a friendship is our own uncertainty that we are valued and accepted. In that fragile attachment to another human, when we question our own value we run the risk of projecting, rightly or wrongly, a false image of our own interest in the relationship. We may even undermine the kindness and commitment we are willing to extend by sending a mixed message that portrays uncertainty rather than interest.

When I look back I wonder how much my anxiety over inadequate language skills was misinterpreted and misunderstood. In the same way that I mistook the facial expressions of women in their doorways in my first country as contempt or animosity, I found I too had been misunderstood.

Sometimes I was caught up in remembering the "rules of culture" I had heard from other people—if I said or did the wrong thing I would be seen as rude or inconsiderate. I probably didn't do those things wrong, but my fear of offending might have sent exactly the opposite signal than what I was hoping for. Sometimes I found that my local friends negated the rules I had been told—either they were outdated or suited to another town. I needed to be willing to make a few more mistakes on the way to sharing myself. It took me a while to learn to be myself and then show kindness and humility when I needed to rebuild after a misunderstanding. One of my coping mechanisms that I'm sure created a wrong impression of my personality was that I retreated into silence far too often.

I love to tell stories, but without the skills in another language to really weave a story, I would often keep silent when we were guests or had guests in our home. Some of our guests were my husband's students, who were earning a degree in English. My silence in these gatherings was not even appropriate, since the students all wanted to practice English. Stories would have benefited their comprehension skills. But I was also worried about overstepping social boundaries, and it felt safer to keep my mouth shut.

Many years after the fact, a student commented on the early visits he had made to our home during his years as a university student. When he first started coming his English was limited and his accent made it hard to understand all that he said. Ironically, his girlfriend was at least as silent as I was. They eventually married each other, and when he got his first job in a country village, we would visit them for weekends; our friendship grew far beyond those early years of teacher-student interactions.

One night over dinner I told a story, creating an atmosphere of anticipation and mystery, letting humour resolve the moment of conflict that every good story wraps into itself. In the encouragement of shared laughter, I might have told several stories—the kids usually liked to request some old stories once we got going.

Into a pause, this former student interjected his observation, saying, "For so many years I thought you were so boring. You never said anything at all."

I had taken so much care to not offend, to not put myself in jeopardy by stepping over social lines, that I had failed to be myself—on nearly every level.

It is very important to know what offends people when you have come to live in their country—I am not saying this is wrong. But being too focused on social norms and protocol is not the best road map for friendship. We don't wish to offend, but observing rules won't help us find our way into people's hearts or invite them into our own.

And really, at the end of the day, the thing that people find most irresistible is when we find joy and delight in them. The warmth that we show and the delight they know that they give us are the promise of a friendship that will grow.

My friendship with Selma didn't end with the terrible mistake I made asking her kids to go home at suppertime one night. I persisted in visiting her, treating her warmly, smiling and enjoying (a pretense, sort of) being with her—even when she was being cold and superior (and probably thinking I was the stupidest woman she had ever met).

One day I was out in my front yard clearing weeds out of my garden. This was a socially strange thing for me to be doing since gardening was not a city woman's job. Selma walked past on her way to the local shop. I had heard from the children that her auntie, a favourite relative who lived nearby, had died. I was still in my special *persona non grata* category, so I had hesitated to go for a visit in order to give my condolences. I was trying to figure out how to show my support in a way that would be meaningful to her.

There was a much lower fence than was normal around the house we rented, so I could see Selma pass by, but she had not seen me near the wall, weeding. I knew she would see me on her way back home, so I got ready for the meeting. I stood up and made my way toward the gate, asking God for the words to say.

As Selma approached, I opened the gate and to my surprise, she walked inside. I fumbled through the unfamiliar territory of giving my condolences in a language I was barely able to toddle through. She looked so sad that I instinctively reached toward her and gathered her into a hug—a comforting, motherly hug. She let go of her reserve and sobbed her sorrow into my shoulder. Tears ran down my face, and we stood there, wet cheeks pressed together in a sadness that broke her icy barriers.

Our friendship was sealed. I was no longer a foreigner, a stranger, or the stupid woman who wouldn't feed her kids. I was her trusted friend—a partner in grief. It isn't actually usual for a woman to hug another woman in grief in that culture, but comfort and tears are a universal language, and she felt my compassion.

My older daughter, who grew up living in and out of Selma's household and then made friends with a new circle of girls when we moved across town, tells me that there comes a point in friendship when you no longer see the culture. Shared sorrows and unspoken pain in such an embrace start to melt and blur the cultural boundaries. The differences between you and the importance of protocol—the "right way" to do and say things—disappear as the other's significance in your own life is established as unshakable.

As surely as Selma had tried to offend me by excluding me from her offer of food to another guest, I had managed to communicate that I valued her despite both my own mistake and her rejection of me. If we can get to this point in a friendship, where someone feels fully secure that we will embrace them even when they have given the proverbial "slap in the face," there is a sound foundation for friendships. These are the friends we choose to share our hearts with.

Another five years would pass with the friendship growing between Selma and me. We moved across town but my efforts to drive over to see her spoke of her value to me. Then one summer, while we were away, she suffered unspeakable tragedy in the loss of both her sons to a collision between their car and a semi-truck. These were the boys who had played for hours in our unfurnished living room, creating scenes of school and war, fun and fantasy, teaching our family the local language and culture. And some days eating our food.

I arrived back in town to the news that the 40-day memorial for Selma's sons would take place that night. It didn't matter what time we arrived, the guests would be seated in her courtyard and along the street where she lived from late afternoon till after midnight—we just had to show up.

We barely saw any of the family that evening as we were among hundreds who came to express support and care. We were fed an elaborate meal and we listened as the Qur'an was chanted by a special band. These rituals marked the end of the period of mourning. After this night, Selma was expected to put the past behind her and move on in the sober expectation that her boys had been welcomed into heaven by her faithfulness to Muslim traditions. Where she had formerly delighted in wearing stylish European clothing, she now dressed in a heavy black robe with a scarf wrapped so tightly around her head that she complained perpetually of a headache—I knew she was hoping this counted for Muslim faithfulness more than the choices of her life before the accident. These new choices might impact the afterlife for her lost sons.

I knew that it would not be possible for Selma to leave those 40 days of mourning and forget the loss of her sons. My life had taught me that losing someone who shares your daily bread—who sits at your table each evening and talks about their day—this kind of loss leaves a gaping hole inside that no manner of faithful service or ritual can fill. She would be mourning this hole for years to come, and she needed permission to do so.

I visited her in the quiet of the next few days when all the relatives had gone, and she was home in silent rooms, alone with all manner of memories. We would talk about the boys, how they had filled my living room with games and laughter in my first months here. These boys were rooted into my own journey with a tangle of good-and-bad memories. But mostly I had loved them as my own family and I mourned with her. Our memories and words were flavoured by our tears, again mixing together.

When the front gate opened and she heard her husband or daughters coming in, or if the bell rang signalling a guest, she would wipe her eyes and say "We must not cry. It is *haram* (forbidden, shameful)." I knew it was *haram*—but when no one else could see, she also knew it was helping her. Tears bring healing, and shared tears much more so than crying alone. Her culture didn't recognize this, but she did. She just wasn't ready to have anyone judge her for breaking the forty-days-of-mourning rule.

The barriers of culture had disappeared between us in the searing need we had for each other as we let go of her sons. For me they represented the key to my family entering into this community—I mourned their loss. For her they were the key to her future—her two daughters would marry and move away but sons would have lived upstairs and brought the joy and laughter of children back into her life as they married and their families grew. They would have provided for her in retirement—her future looked bleak in their absence.

I had respected her culture in many ways, and now in the silent trust of a friendship, I led the way toward healing by allowing her to cry. The cultures had blurred inside the stable walls of our friendship.

In many ways my daughter is more of an expert in blurring of cultures and the removing of barriers than I have been or ever will be. She grew up with her closest friends being our Arab neighbours. She has married someone from another culture and made the effort to build a relationship that understands the differences a culture can make, but defies the divisions it might invite. She has the gift of seeing past culture and into a person's heart because her own heart contains two cultures so securely.

But my daughter's insight about reaching this shifting of barriers resonates with my own experience. Once your heart is opened up to hear the secrets and sorrows and delights in another's heart, the friendship is lifted above the boundaries of culture.

There is no shortcut for getting to this point. The investment of time as well as the necessity of taking each step in the "ladder of connection," building from one to the next, is all part of the process.

TIPS, SUGGESTIONS AND QUESTIONS:

What do your friends like to laugh at? How can you maximize the joy and delight that makes a friendship feel like it is glued together? Even trying out some new words in the new language, and letting people laugh at or with you at your pronunciation is one way to get laughter into your times together. Using your new words or phrases wherever you can, sometimes possibly in awkward or odd ways, can also lead to laughter.

Food often plays a role in the rights of passage—weddings, births, funerals, celebrations. It is important to learn that there are unspoken rules about how this works in each culture, since they can change from village to village.

In the North African country where I lived, there is a ban on sweet food when someone dies—you don't eat cakes or cookies or desserts because this is not a sweet time in your life. If someone wants to bring a gift of food to the family, it would be an insult to give something sweet. It is important to know these things, to avoid the mistakes. In the next country over, this is not the rule, so you have to pay attention and learn the details for yourself.

In some Asian countries there are certain soups that are considered more comforting and therefore what you bring to someone who has experienced a loss. But you would also be remiss if you did not stop and eat the soup with the friend—eating alone during a time of loss is not considered good.

Do you have someone you are friends with who could tell you about how the rituals of grief and death are carried out in their culture? Their insights might help you expand your understanding of how our culture looks to them and you could begin a discussion that leads to greater mutual understanding.

QUESTIONS FOR REFLECTION:

Have you been through a loss in your life that has profoundly changed who you are as a person? How did you find comfort during that time? Was there someone who was comforting to you? What did you learn about offering comfort to others, or how did you become more comfortable sitting with those in grief who need to feel they are not alone?

If you have not had such a loss, do you know someone who has, and could you ask them to share their answers to these questions? How can you learn to be more comfortable around grief so that you are able to sit with those who may be feeling alone?

~ 10 ~

The Gift of Being Seen and Heard

The eternal quest
of the individual human being
is to shatter his loneliness.
Norman Cousins

In North Africa, almost every event we attended was a series of hours of waiting—perhaps for food, perhaps for musicians to arrive, perhaps for a bride. You arrived at a venue or someone's home, and even if it was not a planned event, you had a sense of waiting. People knew how to settle in and be with each other, with or without words. After I got to know a few women, I found it easier to sit—or sit around as we would say. Through the stories that I heard from women, using words as my vehicle for understanding, I came to a recognition that in this culture it was possible to acknowledge people—see them, observe their lives—without understanding the whole story. But my journey toward this understanding began with the opportunities I had to hear the stories.

Meriam had been helping me with cleaning and laundry for about a year when I asked her why she had married Abd al-Qadr, a man who beat her until she went to the police to lay charges. She had given the police my name as a witness to her bruises, so it felt safe, ordinary even, to ask a few questions. She was happy to share her stories. She stayed married to this violent man because otherwise she would have never seen her children again. But she lived in one room of their house, and he lived in the other room, refusing even to eat anything she cooked. The daughters took the job of caring for him, and the family lived in this unpleasant silent arrangement until the arctic freeze between them began to thaw.

In answer to my question, Meriam told me about wanting to leave the village so she could wear city clothes. If she stayed in her village for the rest of her life, she would always wear the heavy country dresses that she disliked. So when her cousin (whom she did not want to marry) started coming around to ask her parents for her hand, she married an unknown city man. She was fifteen when she made this life-altering decision. Her answers gave me a whole new set of insights into the life and culture of country folk.

I asked another friend to tell me what games she had played as a child and again, the answers were not surprising, but the window they gave into her life was remarkable. Before I questioned about her childhood, she had been mostly silent, but as she told these stories she started to edge her way out of her shell and into a world of friendship that included laughter and fun.

Another friend told me about the people in her life who had given her a sense of being treasured—seen and loved. Each time I was startled by how these stories opened my heart to see the soul of a little girl who had grown up to make choices that seemed foreign to me but now made sense.

The gift of listening, and by it observing another person's life, is a profound gift of presence. It may not produce a sweeping change, but it inevitably will change us, most likely in a myriad of small yet profound ways. Each story that is shared about a loss or rejoiced in for the treasure of comforting childhood memories—each moment of gratitude or sorrow—each one has value. As I asked questions, the stories I heard drew me closer to the recognition that every human soul carries the light of the One who created them. To listen and see and understand is to acknowledge the utter value of existence.

These deliberate conversations prepared me for times when I was only briefly a part of a woman's story, and I leaned in to build the friendship through the gift of tears. On several occasions, we encountered loss to death in our community; at these times, words proved inadequate. Once again, presence spoke the message, but tears conveyed my compassion that I hoped brought the gift of healing.

One evening in the summer season of weddings, the lesson of tears was seared into my heart by an encounter with a grief-stricken mother. A few months earlier we had received a call from Hamed, a friend of my husband's, in the middle of the night. Tragically, Hamed's youngest brother, Saleh, had just been killed in a car accident.

My husband left at 3:00am to be with the family who lived nearly three hours away. He came home a few days later, reporting that Hamed's mom, Esma, was beside herself with grief.

Hamed's imminent wedding should have been postponed, as it is considered dishonourable to have a wedding within a year of a family member's death. But Esma was struggling with a crippling form of arthritis and desperately needed a daughter-in-law to help with the household work, which was considerable on their small farm.

The wedding stayed on schedule but was a bizarre, unhappy affair, with a band that would normally play for the event held 40 days after a death. Instead of joyful songs, they performed morose, rhythmic chanting to the beat of various drums. There was no dancing, and Esma and her husband dressed as if they were weeding their potato fields rather than attending a celebration.

My husband had been asked to pick up the band, and then after the wedding events and meal, he drove them home to their village about an hour away. It was already past midnight, and I was settling my youngest daughter to sleep on a mattress in one of the rooms when I heard the sound of a lament coming from the open court in front of their house. I had never heard such a thing before, but I knew immediately by the sound of it that someone was singing a lament.

It was a startling, gripping sound—a voice brimming with emotion. I had heard such a sound in an operatic performance, but this time the emotions were real: profound sadness, deep yearning, and wrenching regret. Only one phrase in all the words was clear enough for me to understand, "Oh God, why have you taken my son from me?"

Without a decision passing through my mind, my feet carried me toward the lamenting mother. Esma's song for Saleh ended just as I reached her, but tears were still streaming down her cheeks. No one had moved to acknowledge her pain—the family stood or sat around the edges of the courtyard in a frozen silence.

My instincts took over, and I pulled Esma into an embrace, leaning her head into my chest, holding her as if I were the mother and she the child. It was a moment born out of my own understanding of deep pain. I stroked her hair and murmured the only words that came to me with clarity, "Jesus, come and heal this pain."

And I cried.

As Esma regained her composure, we moved away from each other without any awkwardness, and she hobbled to the kitchen where family members were cleaning up.

I passed by the kitchen a half hour later, on my way to check on my daughter. Hamed's aunt, Esma's sister, called me in. She began to reprimand me for allowing this lamentation and for crying on a wedding night, long after the time for grieving (40 days) was over. But auntie's tirade was halted by Esma who, hearing the rebuke, answered her sister boldly.

"Don't say that to her. She did what was right. She held me, she cared for me. *I felt her tears on my cheek.* She loves me."

As we drove away that night, just as I closed the van door, I heard Hamed's two nephews begin to wail their own grief for their uncle, Saleh. Their mom told them to stop, but their grandma handed them the gift I had given her, reprimanding her daughter. "Let them cry," Esma said, "they need to grieve." She moved toward them with her arms outstretched.

Tears are not brokenness. And they are not the pain or the problem. Tears are a gift designed for healing the inevitable losses we encounter in life. When we offer the gift of tears, we offer the gift of healing—we all need friends that will sustain the friendship through the valley where those tears are shed. We need to journey through the pain until we get to the other side.

If we have not walked through the valley of tears in our own life, we may not feel comfortable offering this gift to someone from another culture. But more than likely, we have experienced loss and pain, and we will know how to hold a friend's hand and cry with them as they tell their story.

When we look into the life of Jesus, His love for stories gives us that truth—He knew the great value of being present to someone in the story of their loss and healing. We see how much light and truth He brought, over and over, to those He encountered by willingly entering in as a part of their story. This is the grace of a God who has chosen to be with us.

He is here. With us.

No book or curriculum will ever replace the power of a good friend who listens to someone's hard stories and shares their tears. Or someone who waits in silence, sharing the weight of moments that cannot be put into words.

TIPS, SUGGESTIONS AND QUESTIONS:

When you encounter someone who has walked away from the village or city they grew up in, and made their way across the world to a new life, there will be stories. Some of the stories that need to be told will be nostalgic and bring back the comfort and joy of good relationships in childhood. Some of those stories will invite a tsunami of emotion that will feel like it is uprooting the stability of a new life. It is unlikely that telling old stories will shred a new life—the roots were ripped apart years ago and will now only grow deep once again in an environment that offers the gift of being seen and heard.

Having the skill of asking people to tell their stories is more learned by practice than by being told what to ask. Start with some old friends and ask them to tell stories of their life. Anything they remember from a long time ago, anything from childhood, probably contains in it elements that have shaped who they are. Make the effort to ask for those stories and then take the time to reflect on what you have learned through this "window."

Take this skill to your conversations with people from other cultures—be genuine in your curiosity and really get to know them by asking more about their life, about the people and events that have influenced who they have become. Most people love to be seen and heard in this way.

QUESTIONS FOR REFLECTION:

What are your deepest stories? Who are the people who brought you comfort and safety—and how did that shape you? When did you experience fear or loss, and how did you survive those times? Was there someone in your life who was especially good at giving you the feeling that you were seen and heard? How has their acknowledgement of you stayed with you as a gift?

Remember the Poor:

Having come to a rural poor community in North Africa to work with an NGO after a natural disaster 14 years ago, I have been privileged to stay and become part of a close and closed village. Over the course of these years we've had many groups from the West come to assist. I have become more than convinced that what the "poor" want more than anything else is this: to know that they are remembered!

Westerners come and feel the need to "do" something...whereas what these Eastern cousins want more than anything is a visit from the Westerners. They desire (truly like most of us) to have us sit and interact with them. It doesn't matter if we share a language or not! Women and children in particular can find a way to communicate...if you want to enough...and if you are willing to laugh at yourself.

I've been convicted that "to be" with the "poor" is of the utmost importance. How many times does our Book say: Remember the Poor! It doesn't say give everything to them repeatedly, it says Remember... Additionally I am convinced that the elderly, handicapped, and prisoners are also "poor." Orphans and Widows. Remember the Poor! Be with them.

Elie Jo Shaw

~ 11 ~

Made For Family

The problem with our world
is that we draw the circle of family
too small.
Mother Theresa

Before we left Canada to live in North Africa, the last verse in the Old Testament sparked a little campfire in my conscious thoughts that burned there for many months. Like embers glowing at night, these words directed me to consider ideas God was using to form my spiritual journey. This image of God turning hearts of parents toward their children created a fresh awareness for God's tenderness toward my children—and His wish for me to share that.

Look, I am going to send you the prophet Elijah before the great and terrible day of the Lord comes. And he will turn the hearts of fathers to their children and the hearts of children to their fathers. Otherwise, I will come and strike the land with a curse.
Malachi 4:5-6 CSB

The placement of this verse in the Bible struck me—it marked a clean end to the covenant between God and His people based on rules and regulations, do's and don'ts, punishments and requirements. And it signalled the new covenant that was modelled in the life of Christ—a promise of grace, compassion, and the restoration of the friendship between God and humans that was the original offer in the Garden of Eden.

The promise was inserted into the context of family—the deepest, most fundamental human connection. Life has been sustained on this earth through family relationships for centuries. These verses implied that in the new covenant, relationships would be restored with a complete change of hearts between parents and their children. Family, the basic building block of society, would be where redemption worked the promise of transforming cultures.

We began to consider how our family carried the message of restoration and grace in our relationships with each other. As young parents, we tried to become aware of redemption values inside our own home. We wanted to model the radical new representation of God that Jesus had expressed—God as our Dad, *Abba.*

I contemplated this from inside a new cultural paradigm of how family functioned. Loyalty to family relationships was in evidence all around us, challenging me to reconsider how I viewed family. We learned a lot about the value of family relationships from the culture surrounding us.

The term "family" in traditional cultures encompasses more people than it does in our Western, industrialized societies. In the East, "family" automatically includes at least three generations and spans across uncles, aunts, and cousins. One of the natural outcomes is that life has to benefit the whole group. This affects how material goods are viewed as well as how relationships are conducted. For centuries, several generations have lived under the same roof, creating a network of relationships that support and sustain through the toughest of life's cycles—birth and death.

When my friend Naima had her first baby, she told me she wanted to breastfeed, which was not the norm among city women. There were no public health clinics to inform or support her decision, and she wanted information and help. I visited her frequently and gave her the best support I could; she became quite content in the relationship she had with her daughter, which included finding ways to continue breastfeeding when she went back to working full-time hours. She was very committed and resourceful.

Then Naima became pregnant with her second child, much sooner than she had hoped. She wanted to continue breastfeeding, and the idea of doing this while pregnant seemed to overwhelm her. She called me in a state of despair. She sounded like an emotional tsunami had uprooted her best plans. Through tears, she confided that her landlady had urged her toward resolving the issue by having an abortion—a common solution where we lived, though not a public topic of conversation.

As I drove toward her house, I asked myself why she had chosen me to call and talk to about this. Why was she insisting the landlady's advice was a good choice but still weeping with me on the phone? In a country that promoted abortion as a birth control method, she was looking for something from me—permission perhaps? Or for someone to help her stand up against this choice?

I concluded that she must know I was not going to support aborting a baby conceived by parents in a home that was well able to support another child. She must have called because she wanted me to talk her out of this emotionally upsetting decision. I reinforced my resolve with this conclusion that my opposition to the abortion was what she really wanted from me.

Someone recently told me that when there is a disagreement, the person with the most certainty is the one who will win. I knew certainty was on my side. I was sure that Naima would regret the decision if she aborted this baby. So we talked it through, and the guy who said certainty wins is right.

Naima tried to convince me that my opinion was irrelevant to her context. She told me, as if she knew my history personally, "You don't understand. You had your mother there to help you when you had babies. You had your sister. You were not alone. I will be alone—my mom is too old to come help. And my sister can't help me, she is too busy with her studies." Naima had no idea that my mom and sister were nowhere near me when my babies were born. She assumed we lived in the same paradigm of family as she did—family would surround anyone in need. She was the anomaly in her culture because of her circumstances.

Traditionally in that culture, Naima would have been surrounded by female relatives who would provide food for her and take care of the house. But in our modern city, she had moved across town and lived alone with her husband and child in an apartment.

All my arguments about the sacred gift of life and the blessings of children did little to persuade Naima. But when she accepted my offer to pray, her emotions returned to a calm stability, and she accepted this child within her. We prayed a second prayer, a blessing on this baby, and it occurred to me that I could help.

I could pay for the lady that cleaned my house to come clean and cook for her throughout the summer months. I knew it would be desperately hard for Naima to keep up her household chores in 45C heat. This gave my cleaning lady employment for the summer months. In offering this, I filled the gap that Naima had been expressing concern about.

The importance of this offer was made clear to me on the day Naima gave birth to her son. As I sat in her hospital room throughout the day, while relatives came and went, I heard again and again what this gesture meant to her.

Naima told each of her guests, "This is my Canadian friend, the one I told you about. She is the reason Hassan is here. She sent her cleaning lady to help me last summer when I thought I wouldn't make it."

I had become her family in that event, and since her mother's reason for not helping was poor health, I offended no one. It was considered a gift to the whole family.

There is nothing better that you can do for a North African woman than treat her like family. If she is far from her parents and siblings, she is alone. This is how that culture sees this—if you are without your extended family, you are alone.

One time my next-door neighbour told me in all seriousness that she understood exactly how I felt living so far from my family. She knew how hard it was to be alone, she said—her family lived 156 kilometres south of us. I nearly laughed out loud, thinking this was a funny comparison, but as I walked the 30 yards from her gate to mine, I realized it was true—she felt isolated and alone without her sisters and mom in and out of her life every day. She understood better than I had realized!

When we first moved abroad, we naturally tried to find other Westerners who shared our faith and holiday traditions to spend Christmas and Easter with. Usually we invited an American single mom and her son for several nights, along with another family or two. We enjoyed familiar traditions together—our Christmas tree, carols, and the food I carefully planned with special ingredients from abroad. We created family for each other around special times that drew us deeply into the roots of our home culture.

One year as I was preparing for the Christmas Eve meal (our turkey dinner), the phone rang, and two of my husband's former students gleefully announced that they were on their way. Their bus had just left their station, and they would be at our house in about three hours. "We know it is your feast so we are coming," they declared in a tone that anticipated our delight at their arrival.

I had made preparations for food our local friends would enjoy the following day and was reserving this evening for our foreign "family." I fretted about how I would find beds for two more guests since everyone else was sleeping at our house as well. Suddenly I realized what a great honour it was that our former students had recognized our lack of family and were stepping into the gap. They were blessing us with their company and indicating that they were our family.

They stayed for three days, and on Boxing Day, the wife offered to cook. With my daughters helping her find things in the kitchen, there was a great deal of laughter cooked straight into that meal. I enjoyed a night off and an exceptional meal. It was indeed a family affair.

Family ties were extremely strong where we lived—loyalty was decidedly linked to putting family first. In instances of conflict, loyalty went to family before it went to friends. Sometimes that meant no matter how much we had invested, we could not be absolutely sure we would be prioritized or defended. This felt, at times, like we were "at risk," which was not comfortable for us.

When we refused to lend our DVD player to one of the student's roommates, we saw this division of loyalties first hand. A group of about 15 students had come to our home several times for movie nights, so for Thanksgiving I invited them to share our special meal. One of the students had a roommate whom we'd never met. The roommate asked to borrow our DVD player that night (which we said no to because of the party), but we invited him to bring the movie and view it with friends in our house another time.

As I was putting the finishing touches on the special dinner, one student rang the bell, stood outside the gate, and explained to my husband how offensive this refusal had been. He excused himself from attending our Thanksgiving feast, making a shallow apology and explaining that he was obligated to show loyalty to his roommate. I sat on the floor in the kitchen and cried before pulling myself together and serving the meal to the few who had come—the story had been shared before the event, and only three people showed up for dinner. Being from a different part of the country, those three were not obliged to show loyalty to the roommate.

We had to persist in giving our best, opening our hearts and homes generously, and expressing how much we valued the relationship. It was crucial for us to recognize that any loyalty we showed to our local friends was of immense value, even when it didn't feel that way. This was part of what had rebuilt my friendship with Selma my first years in town.

At times it felt that this cultural bias was a one-way avenue to loyalty—we had to prove our dedication but never expect we were secure in a relationship. Family ties would trump our friendship if there was any competition. But that would be the expectation toward us, as well—that if our family needed something, we would prioritize those needs over the friendship. In our Canadian culture, loyalty is not automatically given to family members. Sometimes friends who have "earned" it get our allegiance ahead of relatives.

We were fortunate to learn this value of prioritizing family for ourselves, first hand. The value on family relationships is a clear theme throughout Scripture, but nowhere more powerfully expressed than in the words of Paul—

When the time came to completion, God sent his Son, born of a woman, born under the law, to redeem those under the law, so that we might receive adoption as sons. And because you are sons, God sent the Spirit of his Son into our hearts, crying, "Abba, Father!" So you are no longer a slave but a son, and if a son, then God has made you an heir. Galatians 4:4-7 CSB

In the invitation of the Gospel we are clearly accepted into God's family as full members. When we understand what the powerful bonds of family connection mean to other cultures, this verse blooms with deep significance. The connection between redemption and adoption is clear. We are being redeemed back into the family relationship that God had in mind when He created humanity.

The heart of the Gospel message is that we are invited into a relationship with God as our "Dad"—when Jesus called His father "*Abba,*" this was a radical new image of how to relate to God. We have lost many layers of this message by living in a culture where family relationships are treated as optional and relatives so often live in isolation from each other.

My experience taught me there is nothing better than having a sense of family in a new land. At first that family feeling comes more easily from those of similar language and culture, but over time, as the culture shock passes, it is a treasured gift to have local friends who embrace you as their kin—nearest and dearest. This sense of being family with them is surely one of the bridges we build that gives greater access to the invitation into the Kingdom.

TIPS, SUGGESTIONS AND QUESTIONS:

One of the features of the cultures we lived in was that people would always ask me how my family in Canada was doing. They may not ask how I was doing—but for sure they would ask about my dad. Was he in good health? And if a friend or neighbour knew I had a sister, they would ask about her health and her children as well.

This is one of the ways that you can easily start a conversation that may lead to friendship—we all have a family to talk about. When you meet someone from another culture, ask about their relatives: parents, siblings, aunts, uncles. Remembering to ask how they are doing when you see them again is a big deal.

If you are building a friendship with a refugee family, they may be facing the deep loss of family. Hearing their story is a gift of kindness and compassion. Listen for what family and loyalty means to them, and be ready to show you are faithful to the friendship.

Likewise, knowing how to ask about the need for family here in Canada is important. You may not have the time to fully fill the gap, so be careful that you don't label yourself as their new family unless you feel sure you understand what that means to them and are sure you will be able to live up to their expectations. It is better to underpromise and overdeliver than vice versa.

QUESTIONS FOR REFLECTION:

What history of family belonging and loyalty do you carry? Was this a strong value in your home? Is this a value you wish had been a bigger part of your own family growing up? Is it something you would like to grow in now?

What comes to mind when you consider the various Scriptures about family relationships from Malachi's and Paul's writings? Upon reflection, do you have a desire to learn more deeply what it means to be inside the faithfulness offered by God as your Father?

My Boy:

In the rural community where I've lived for the past decade the women give birth in the hospital but no one is allowed in to be with them. I shared a house with a very young woman who had been married just a year, when the time came to give birth to her first born. She was very nervous and scared of the whole process. A crowd of family and friends took her to the hospital but when shooed away by hospital staff everyone was ready to return to our neighbourhood an hour away. I couldn't stand the thought of all of us so far away in case something happened and she needed someone who loved her with her. So I decided to spend the night in my truck parked outside the hospital…a female relative decided to stay with me (we ended up on a friend's couch just down the block from the hospital).

I called the young mom multiple times on our new-fangled cell phones to see how she was. First thing in the early morning I returned to the hospital and when visiting hours were over I stayed with her, helping her, walking with her, and encouraging her. I stayed until some member of the hospital staff shooed me away….but only when they directly asked. I boldly did not make eye contact often as this kept them from asking me to leave. I stayed right outside the hospital and returned as soon as they allowed visitors again.

This happened repeatedly through the day and each time I was able to stay longer, as I was actually helpful, and they could tell I wanted to stay. So when it came time for her active labor I had to leave the room as our foreign doctor friend had arrived and could assist the midwife in case of emergency. The security guy for that floor told me to leave…but I said please in his mother tongue…and looked so pathetic (as it had been over 20 hours at this point-and he knew I'd been there most of that time) he took pity and let me go in an empty room across the hall. Minutes later I saw the little blue boy being weighed by the nurse and went right back in! What joy for this over 40 single woman!

When we finally got home from the hospital with baby and momma both extended families welcomed me with open arms. They repeatedly told everyone how I refused to leave the hospital and even when the staff made me, I only went outside. To my surprise they told this as if I were a hero! In my view it was something anyone would do for someone they loved, but for them it was HUGE. I have been treated as family ever since this sweet day.

Elie Jo Shaw

~ 12 ~

Ten Carrots

Don't judge each day
by the harvest you reap
but by the seeds you plant.
Robert L. Stevenson

When we moved overseas, we knew we were called to be a light wherever we lived. We wanted to earn a living in a country that needed more spiritual light, but it wasn't our first intention to start a church there. However, God had other plans, and we ended up catching a vision for something bigger than we had imagined.

There were subtle and sometimes obvious expectations from church leaders or mentors on how we should be spending our time and reporting our activities. During those first seven years, I found myself drifting more and more toward a performance emphasis in my faith as an activity that could be measured. I was encouraged to report how many conversations I had about Jesus. I needed to account for my time and justify that I was productive enough.

I grew increasingly frustrated with my "results." It had slipped my mind that in my journey towards an overseas life of faith, God had impressed on me that my first calling was to my own family—to be a mom. My other calling or vocation, which could be woven seamlessly with the first one, was to pray. But even prayer could be turned into a results-based performance, and I was feeling that pressure—what were the results when I prayed? Who did I share my faith with? How did they respond?

I began to feel like I was banging my head against a brick wall, trying to create interest in conversations where curiosity and invitation were lacking. My efforts to ignite spiritual hunger in people around me were fruitless. As I shared this frustration with God, this "headache" resulting from repeatedly hitting a wall, it occurred to me that walls were an important motif in the Scriptures. Prophets were given walls for their symbolic meanings; sometimes walls came down in order to reveal a spiritual reality.

I began to ask God more about the meaning of walls—in particular, the purpose of this barrier, *my wall*. I set myself to wait on God's Spirit to reveal understanding through reading and reflection on Scripture. Occasionally people would comment on the subject of spiritual walls in a conversation, and their insights would confirm what I felt God was saying. One of those comments came very clearly through a book I picked up in a friend's house; the author pointed out that praise and worship are our strongest weapons of spiritual warfare, based on the story of Jericho. I had been contemplating how worship had proved powerful yet without force, in bringing down the walls of Jericho.

Reading the first chapter on the topic of worship bringing down walls was a wonderful moment of confirmation. I had come to North Africa with a clear vocation to pray, yet I had grown dissatisfied that prayer alone was enough. The idea that prayer preceded a spiritual shift was a reminder of that first calling. Additionally, my prayers were most powerful when they came from a place of praise. This was the key I had been looking for.

I began praise walking—my own version of prayer walking. Instead of asking for things, I spent the walking time focused on how great God already was, how His Kingdom was my delight, and how the mercy and grace I had received was abundant and fulfilling.

I praise walked back and forth to the vegetable stand almost every day. It was only about two hundred meters—out my gate, across an empty lot, and then across a main street in our section of town. There sat an older man, the vegetable seller, with a few boxes of vegetables and some herbs for sale. He was faithfully available from dawn until after sunset when working women had cooked the evening meal.

The veggie man's scale sat on a makeshift counter where he also kept a half-sharp knife for cutting pumpkins or slicing off the greens after the vegetables were weighed. Customers paid for all the greens and then he cut them off and threw them in a pile for a shepherd to collect. I took mine home and threw them in the hole we made in the garden for easy composting, feeding worms. These trips fed not only my family but my favourite hobby as well—my flower garden.

I was quite happy to contribute to this man's livelihood. If my husband drove into town for vegetables, he would likely find fresher produce, but I wanted to support this veggie seller who was always honest with his math. I'd been ripped off by enough merchants that I was enthusiastic about supporting the honest ones.

Though we never learned each other's names, or gained a friendship through words, the sense of belonging grew between us. He wrote each price down for me to see and then added the sum, carefully and slowly. When he got the total wrong it was usually in my favour. I would add it up again for him and give him the correct amount. This didn't offend him and contrasted with my experience with the other vegetable seller on the main road who was slick with his numbers but seemed to add about a dollar bonus for himself each time.

I had tacitly built a relationship of trust with this faithful gentleman who served our community. I enjoyed watching him lay the vegetables carefully on one side of his scale, matching the other side with a chunk of metal that balanced the weight. He did his work with focused precision. Sometimes he would throw a little weight onto the vegetable side to counter a too-heavy weight on "his" end. This little ritual reminded me of my childhood when I bought candy measured on a similar scale in a tiny shop in South America. Perhaps this added to my joy in visiting the veggie man's little trading post.

After paying for my veggies and packing them into my basket, I would walk home with my purchases. I could turn my thoughts toward planning what these veggies could produce for supper or continue with my praise walking.

Gradually, without an identifiable moment of revelation, I noticed that carrots, my favourite vegetable, resembled the shape of people. The heavy kilo weight on the other side had to represent something else—something that symbolized my life, the weight of my being here in this desert city.

"Years," I thought to myself. "The kilo weight represents years that I have spent here in this country."

I began a conversation with God that would take nearly two years to complete. It coincided with the time that I was frustrated with banging my head against a brick wall, spilling over into the time I spent praise walking—both of these held clues as to what God was doing in me. He was moving me out of my frustration with results back into my calling in prayer.

This conversation emerged into the clarity of a specific question:

If I had known that I would give ten years of my life (this decade mark was three years away), and the "product" would be only ten people who would know Christ personally as their saviour, would I have made that sacrifice at the outset? Would ten years of my time "weigh up" with the outcome of just ten people coming to know Christ? Would I have come if I had known that was all it was worth?

I was not sure that I would have made the choice for that exchange. I could not honestly say yes to this.

I needed to settle the disappointment in my soul. And yet, I still had three years to go—perhaps in three years we would see this as our result. Was this something I should be asking God for, interceding as Abraham did for his city? Negotiating a fair weight? Ten years of my life for the result of ten people choosing to follow Jesus?

Days of praying this conversation turned to months, and I was still uncertain. My daily walk to buy vegetables and the sight of a bunch of carrots on a scale reminded me that I didn't have an answer to the question. I kept praying, contemplating, waiting—for insights. How should I pray?

Into this space, where an answer would have been welcomed, I began asking this question instead: *What would make it worth a whole "kilo" of my life to live here?* As we drew close to a year of this slow transformation from frustration to praise, I was ready to ask myself if my "kilo" would be worth just seven people, seven carrots for my "kilo" on the other side of the scale?

And then I was ready to ask if three was enough. We were possibly going to be in the ballpark of three people at the mark of one decade, it seemed. Was I willing to give—to have given—ten years if only three people chose to follow the Gospel? In my hesitance, I felt the Spirit tugging at my heart to consider something new.

As I continued to walk and pray, one day God gave me the answer. It came in the form of a picture, like a photograph that flashed through my memory—something I had seen once and remembered. Maybe a scale in the markets of Marrakesh, somewhere old and traditional. Some place I had not been in reality, only in my imagination. But it was a clear picture. On that scale, on the customer side, my side, there were *no vegetables—no carrots at all.*

There was a tall tapering pile of seeds, looking much like a mountain. A mountain of seeds—too many to count.

We were not being given carrots for our kilo, not really. We were being given seeds. We could use these seeds as freely as we wished; they seemed to number in the thousands. The parable of the sower, as told by Jesus as a picture of the Gospel message, began to impact me in new ways as I considered what it meant to be the carrier of His seeds.

Intuitively I knew that the seeds represented our prayers and the opportunities we were given to care about and for people. The Gospel could not be separated from the seeds of hope and love—not in our lives in this city, it seemed. Not that I want to separate prayer and care, because over these years it had become clear to me that caring for people is a form of prayer. Just as much as praise and intercession are forms of prayer, weeping with those who weep, offering cups of tea, piling plates high with couscous, glasses of water to boys at my gate—these were all opportunities to live our prayers as surely as we uttered them in words.

And so my life was steered back to the vocation I had identified prior to coming here. I was here to pray. I needed to pray. I might not see the results other people recognized and acknowledged. I came to terms with that.

But I needed my prayers to change someone, and without a shadow of a doubt, the first person they were changing was me.

TIPS, SUGGESTIONS AND QUESTIONS:

We all have a purpose in life—a place of influence that God has put us for the greater good and for the glory of His kingdom. If you have not considered how your purpose might include being a blessing to the nations, the stories in this book might be calling you to consider that—it is the first "purpose" of our Christian faith, as it was the reason God called Abraham to become the father of faith.

Abraham is considered the father of other faiths as well—Judaism and Islam. There are many ways that we can consider ourselves a blessing to people of other "nations" or cultures, and ways that they can be a blessing to us too.

Take time to consider how you can put this purpose of being a blessing into practice in your life—both for friends you already have and for new friends from backgrounds different than your own. If your primary motivation is to bless them, the door will be that much easier to open on a friendship.

QUESTIONS FOR REFLECTION:

What is your primary purpose in life? Have you spent time considering this? If you are invested in fulfilling the purposes that God has for you, then you might be facing challenges, but overcoming those should be giving you a deep sense of satisfaction. Do you have friends who share those purposes? How can you make sure that you have enough community with those who understand and share those purposes so that you can stay motivated and intentional in pursuing them?

~ 13 ~

Telling Old Stories

Be a fountain,
Not a drain.
Rex Hudler

I went back to work part-time when my children were in middle school. I didn't know if I wanted the job, but the university department head decided for me.

My husband had worked in the English department for eleven years, dealing with a complexity of political rules and cultural expectations. Although I had a master's degree, I was not tempted to join him on the teaching faculty, and until "Nicole" came to teach for a year, no one knew I had such a degree of education.

Nicole decided I would be an asset to the department and invited us to a dinner with the department head. The dinner turned into a recruiting meeting where I was pressured to take on a teaching role. To keep myself from sounding "ill bred"—to avoid that disgrace, I agreed to "think about it." I actually had zero wish to start teaching in the atmosphere I had heard so much about.

The department head announced to the dean that I would be replacing Nicole, teaching full time in the Fall semester. It would have sounded like I was going back on a commitment which would have landed on my husband's reputation if I now refused, so I agreed to teach half time. My husband reassured me that I only had to go for a couple of weeks to try it out before making a final decision—but the young women in my classes won my heart on my first day.

From week to week I would prepare for teaching grammar (not my favourite), and think of interesting exercises that might spark imaginative conversations. I also came prepared to tell a story from my life after the break between two long sessions—it was a three hour class, scheduled in two different buildings, so it was tempting for students to leave for the day after the first half. Except they knew there would be a story. The students waited for these stories, reminding me if I appeared to bypass that segment of the class. I suspected many of them would skip the second half of the weekly lesson if I put the story before the break!

I struggled to learn all my students' names. I had prided myself in my 20s that I could identify three or four classes of 20 students from one week to the next, recalling their names by memory. Now in my forties, I only had two classes of about 35 students in total, and I struggled.

When I called one of the sharper students by the wrong name, her blunt correction—"My name is *Hejer*, Miss,"—had more than a tinge of exasperation in it.

Then it occurred to her to give me the clue I needed to remember her name—"Like the mother of Ishmael. You know, *Hejer*." It was, indeed, a useful clue, as I had not identified her with this woman from the story of Abraham.

Living for 12 years in North Africa had given me a great regard for Hagar. I had often glossed over her story, missing the nuances of God's blessing on her life—until I lived in this context. Hagar had become quite real to me as one of God's people.

"Oh," I said, "I love that story. *Hejer* is one of my favourite women of faith."

It was an English class, but we often took digressions into topics of spiritual values. I was comfortable discussing my life of faith in ways that would not alienate my students, and they were eager to hear from my experiences which must have sounded exciting. Most of them had never left the little provincial city we lived in. I often talked about "my faith community" and "your faith community." I would look for things that would draw us together, build the commonality, and give them reasons to trust me. It had started when they asked me why I lived in that city, and my answer included the things I admired about their community. I had told them what I was learning from their culture, and they begged to hear more.

I could have shut the door on these faith discussions by telling them how I disagreed with their faith. I could have majored on the things I deemed missing or ways I thought their religious activity compromised the values it claimed to hold. That would have ended the dialogue.

I think we are all somewhat the same that way. Our faith, whether we call it a faith or a religion or a personal value system, is very important to us. When we see someone approaching who might be here to convince us that we are wrong, we tend to close off a door to our hearts. We might be polite enough to listen for a few moments, but there is no chance of a friendship building out of those encounters. I know when I see a Mormon or Jehovah's Witness coming down my street, my inner response is not very welcoming.

I was aiming for the opposite kind of dialogue with my students. So when *Hejer* told me her name, I jumped into the opportunity to admire the original bearer of that name. I talked about how much Hagar had to rely on God—how her circumstances had forced her to look to God. This drew out the theme of the sovereignty of God, which Christians and Muslims hold in common, though with differences. I continued by commenting on how unique she was as the only woman recorded for giving God a name. It was and is a profoundly insightful name—"the God who sees." I spoke about how every one of us wants to be seen and known, and that this name for God was one of my favourites.

I could see that *Hejer*'s disdain toward me for my forgetfulness was softening in my enthusiasm and knowledge of the woman whose name she bore.

I asked a few questions as I shared these ideas, and finding that the students actually knew very little about Hagar, I paused to consider how much more I could share. I decided to mention the water of life that the angel came to show her. At least, that is how I hear the story—Hagar was the original "woman at the well." Outcast and alone in the desert, she hid her son under a prickly bush so that wild animals wouldn't attack him as he was dying. Hagar fully expected Ishmael to die, but when she turned away from him, a supernatural being showed her a source of water which saved both Hagar and Ishmael from death.

Living in a desert landscape, my students and I appreciated the importance of that water. The power in the story needed no further explanation to us. The seeds of the Gospel message were planted in this moment—the revelation of the well, the water of life. It wasn't the moment to explain the connection to Jesus, but the seeds were there, planted.

As much as it was welcomed that I should talk about my faith community in the context of a conversational class, it was equally appalling to them that I might try to use the opportunity to confront them with my religion. I had to let the seeds lie, perhaps deeply planted, and cultivate the conditions that I could for them to sprout. I also had to trust that the Spirit of God would faithfully cultivate these seeds to life.

This was a principle I had learned to respect. We can drive people away from the next conversation if we step over the invisible line of respect in the current conversation. Or we can invite them to a love for the story and the meaning of the story if we don't push their faces into something they are not ready for. We have to lean on the leading of the Holy Spirit and trust that He is competent to do the part that is His job, not ours.

Most of the Old Testament heroes of our faith are considered prophets by Muslims. We can start with Adam and the story in the Garden of Eden and work our way through any number of stories. Some people specialize in telling these stories in chronological order, asking for feedback at the end of each one as to the spiritual truth or point of that story. With good dialogue, the listener should be able to come to some of his or her own conclusions. For example, God was eager to provide and save Hagar from death in that encounter in the desert. By nature God generously offers us salvation.

If we move to Noah, we add to the story that God is not pleased with unrighteousness but again (as in Hagar's story) He offers a way of salvation from death for those who obey him.

My personal experience of sharing these stories has been rather random, and I am not a specialist in asking probing questions that get the listener to tell me the main spiritual truth. I've found that people enjoy talking about the prophets, but I've also discovered that many women don't know the details of these stories. Where I lived, women were often content to let their husbands be the devoted Muslims and guardians of their faith.

Even so, most people we met were willing to have a conversation about the prophets. An enthusiastic presentation of the wonderful insights you can find in these stories is hard to resist. Stories are the universal carrier of truth because they appeal to our inner structures that make sense of life. Stories of struggle and triumph, of brokenness and redemption carry themes common to all our lives. Truth is a light, even when we didn't realize we were walking in the dark.

From the premise that all people will be glad for a light on their pathway, it is not hard to have conversations about the Old Testament stories. The purpose of the stories found in the Old Testament is that they all bear some light, something of truth that points toward the Gospel. Woven together, they are like signposts that create a journey toward a destination—the revelation of Jesus as the Lamb of God, Saviour and Redeemer.

One day I went to pray at a public square in our city, beside one of the biggest shrines in North Africa. These shrines, also known as saint's tombs are a common spiritual site in many Muslim countries. This one was a popular destination for people who wanted a blessing on some event (a wedding, a birth, or even their studies) in their life. It was also known as a place for sick people to get prayer for healing. I didn't go inside the building that housed the tomb but sat down at a bench in the shade. I was there with the friend who had motivated this prayer time. She was visiting from a neighbouring country and recognized that this tomb was a spiritual power point for all of North Africa, not just this city. She and I prayed and asked God to reveal how He wanted us to pray for this place on this day.

As my friend got up and moved away toward the places she had decided to pray, I hardly had 60 seconds to contemplate or listen further for God's direction. Walking toward me, dressed from head to toe in a dull shade of brown even down to the gloves on her hands, was a young "covered" woman. With one glance at her clothing, I knew she was serious about her devotion to God. The colour of her apparel, the lack of ornamentation and make-up, and the gloves all bore the same message of sincere Islamic faith and piety.

She politely asked if she could sit next to me, and I welcomed her with a cordial greeting that conveyed more than just a polite "hello." When she shared her name, we commented on the meaning—"Faith"—which she assured me was very precious to her. I wanted to say, "I know, I can see by your clothing that your faith guides your life." But instead I fed the conversations with genuine curiosity—how had she come to such a sincere faith? What did that mean to her? By the time she left a half hour later, she was kissing my cheeks on both sides with the warmth reserved for friends.

What ensued in the time between Faith's arrival and departure was a conversation that convinced her I was someone she could trust and wanted to "belong with"—the basis of friendship. We started by talking about the saint's tomb, and I asked her to tell me why she had come there. I expected to hear a personal reason, but instead Faith gave me a generic answer about why most people came (I already knew that, but didn't tell her); then she said, "I am meeting a friend here."

"Yes, I am that friend," I thought to myself. I had just asked God for His plan for my next hour, and I was sure it was here, in this conversation.

We moved on to a deeper topic through the door I opened with my next question. Faith had already mentioned her devotion to God. So I asked which of the prophets was her favourite. I was on safe ground here because I knew Faith was probably going to share a name I was familiar with from the Old Testament. Muslims and Christians share a regard for many of the same "fathers of faith," though we would not call all of them prophets.

Her favourite was Joseph, who is also one of my many favourites. I let my face light up with joy as she mentioned his name and affirmed her choice. The word "favourite" doesn't actually imply exclusivity in my mind, which is handy when I am feeling enthusiastic!

Faith shared what she liked about Joseph, and I shared some of my favourite lessons from his life as well. As I talked about the dreams Joseph experienced as a means of hearing from God, I noticed a puzzled look on her face. I asked if she knew that his dreams had resulted in giving him favour in the king's eyes. Dreams had led to the famous job he had as overseer of preparations for the predicted famine, thus saving the Egyptian nation from starvation in a drought.

Faith admitted she knew nothing about Joseph's dreams, so I gladly shared the details, stressing how important dreams can be as we search out our pathway with God. This is already a favoured means to understanding God among many Muslims, so I was not being controversial. I suggested that if she asked, God would give her dreams as well, while praying in silence that the Holy Spirit would use dreams to speak to her.

Our time closed with my curiosity driving me to ask how Faith would like me to pray for her and her country. She had no qualms about sharing a personal family request with me, and I related how I would pray for that in light of the conversation we had just shared around the prophet Joseph—there is no good reason, in my mind, to deny his status as a prophet. He certainly lived a life that prophetically pointed to Jesus.

As Faith shared her wish for her nation, my heart was moved. It is amazing how deeply a personal dream or desire can stir another person toward compassion and genuine connection. My conversation with Faith had moved quickly from the things we shared in common—a deep regard for spiritual matters, to a sense of belonging to a common cause, to significance in each other's hearts.

The time had passed for Faith's rendezvous with her friend. She took out her phone and found the friend had been waiting in another location. Someone had gone to the wrong place, and I knew it wasn't me. Faith apologized that she needed to move on quickly. As I watched her walking away, I recognized that I had just planted my one seed into her life. By prayer I could nurture that seed and expect God to do the work of bringing germination.

If Faith had asked me to meet again, or if I had sensed any urgency in my spirit to carry on the conversation, I would have suggested she take my phone number. But on this sunny day, in the shadow of the palms that protected a dead saint, I felt confident that there would be others who would find their way into Faith's journey with stories of truth from the One who left his tomb empty.

TIPS, SUGGESTIONS AND QUESTIONS:

In the beginning of the chapter, I talked about getting roped into teaching at the university. What might have contributed to how I felt this choice would reflect badly on my husband? Were there some cultural clues there?

The student, Hejer, seemed annoyed that I had not remembered her name. In what way might that be a cultural cue? How did I repeat the themes of the story of Selma? Was there something else I could have done—or do you see cultural options there?

In this chapter, the clothing of "Faith" is described as being a part of her expression of devotion to God. Our apparel and other aspects of our physical behaviour can create a very strong first impression on people around us, without us taking this in at a conscious level. Pay attention to the clothing you and your friends wear and try to see it through the eyes of someone from another culture—what message are you sending? Is it the one you want to send?

Now pay attention to the clothing that is worn by people from other cultures. Do they dress up for some occasions more than others? Is there a particular standard that they hold to? If you have a friend from another culture ask her some questions about this topic and see what you can learn.

QUESTIONS FOR REFLECTION:

How well do you know the stories of the Bible? Can you tell them without having to look them up—in a way that captures the imagery and the essence of what is inspiring? When would you have opportunities to tell these stories so that they can become part of your dialogue and inspire people around you?

~ 14 ~

Speaking of Jesus

Don't shine so others can see you.
Shine so that through you
others can see Him.
C.S.Lewis

If you are not reading this book from a personal perspective of Christian faith, parts of this chapter may not be pertinent to you. In that case, you might have other things you want to share with friends of other faiths or cultures—values or causes that matter to you, so the principles might be useful.

If you are reading this from a perspective of feeling the *need to share* your faith with people of different cultural and faith backgrounds, then this is definitely for you. As I suggested previously, if we share without understanding the perspective our audience comes from, we run the risk of chasing them away from the conversation—and the friendship. Barriers are often easier to put up than friendships are to build or repair.

The Scriptures that prophesy the coming of Christ are full of references to the "clearing away of rocks"—making the pathway ready. The friendships that we develop with people of other faiths should include this very important task of taking down the barriers that might turn them away from faith or make it difficult for them to make the journey.

When we look back at the "roadmap" to friendship given in chapter two, the same principles come back to help us. We can start with the things we hold in common and build on the principles and values that are shared between our faiths and cultures. This will establish a much stronger foundation than going immediately to the things we know are going to be different—things that may cause misunderstanding and distance between us. A lot of Western Christians feel they have to focus exclusively on what is different in the other faith. If we stop to consider this for just a minute, it is easy to see our own reaction to people who do this.

I don't know about you, but sometimes I run out my back door when I see the Mormons coming down the street. I admire my husband who is able to manage the encounter with both grace and honesty—letting them know he won't be considering their website, but still being polite and kind. Still, the barrier is up because we know they have one agenda and we are determined not to be moved by them. I'm secretly afraid they are going to harass me for the things they believe I have gotten wrong, so I avoid the conversation. I don't want anyone ever to feel that way about me.

I don't know as much about the Hindu, Sikh, and Buddhist faiths as I do about Islam. In the Islamic faith, many Christians assume that there is no knowledge or respect given to Christ. In fact, there are enough truths in the Qur'an that are shared in the Bible that some Muslims have come to believe that Christ is the Messiah (a person Muslims are waiting for) just from their own study of the Qur'an.

It is worth investing in understanding the faith of the friends we are making. If we want to know more about their faith—*ask them!* I know this sounds rather obvious, but it is surprising how often it is skipped over. By showing respect and interest in how a person's faith guides their life, we are building understanding and mutual honour. We will likely find that this stage will establish a sense of belonging. This kindness and respect is a solid invitation for them to hear what we have to say, too. It is important to have a sense of belonging and shared values before we move on to the friendship stage of significance, which is where we can disagree on important things but still be friends.

When sharing our beliefs about Christ, there are two passages from the Bible that I believe should inform our approach to people of other cultures and faiths.

But honour Christ as Lord in your hearts. Always be ready to give a defense to anyone who asks you for a reason for the hope that is in you. 1 Peter 3:15. CSB

This instruction—to honour Christ as Lord—implies a sense of respect for how Jesus lived as well as respect that we acknowledge Christ as the Lord and creator of all people and cultures. Treating others with respect is part of honouring the Lordship of Christ.

The second phrase instructs us to give an answer *when you are asked.* It follows that waiting to be asked for the reasons behind our faith is a respectful way to approach the topic. If we build an honest friendship with someone of another faith, it stands to reason that eventually—if they feel loved and cared for—they will ask about our beliefs. This may not happen if they sense we have no interest or respect for their beliefs—but an honest dialogue is a normal result of mutual respect.

The third phase in this text says, "give a reason for the hope that is in you." It isn't an imperative to give every argument in favour of our own theological stance. It is about the hope that lives inside of our own soul—how did we get there, how are we growing in this?

According to the declaration that initiated Jesus' time as a Rabbi (the reading of Isaiah 61 in the synagogue), His work is to "heal the broken hearted and set the captive free." If we can share how Jesus has done these things for us—healed our hurts and set us free of thoughts or behaviours that have held us in captivity—we may be surprised at the reception.

There was a time in my life when I shared the concept of Christ as healer and redeemer from a "theoretical" perspective. I had not actually experienced any kind of emotional healing, and I was not free of the bondage of hidden brokenness within me. I was not aware of all that I had buried deep in my soul—it was too deep to talk about.

Through a series of events, I became aware of my profound need for healing and freedom. Of course, this was disclosed just as God was opening new avenues of ministry for healing and deliverance. It was God's timing that brought me to a season of healing.

As this healing unfolded, the Gospel message took on a new power in my life. Deeply buried sorrows were exposed and healed, and patterns of anger and fear were broken. The faith I had in Christ took on a new dimension, and I was able to share with confidence that if we ask Jesus to heal a deep heart wound, He will certainly do so.

I also came to understand that it was through healing of a buried pain that forgiveness became attainable. I had tried for years to forgive those who had wounded me during my childhood years. Many times I had made the choice to forgive, waiting for the feelings of forgiveness to follow. But I was deeply wounded by events beyond my control, and the pain was buried so deep it was not affected by my choice to forgive.

While we were living in North Africa, I encountered some people who taught that these buried wounds could be released and healed by prayer that drew me into the presence of Jesus. I was finally set free of the darkness, and the effects of forgiveness became evident in my life.

A young couple came to visit us one day, unable to move forward in their own relationship because of something the young man had done. The woman acknowledged it was her lack of forgiveness that was holding them back. She wanted to forgive, but could not. I offered to pray for her, but told her I would pray for Jesus the healer to touch her deep hurt. She agreed to this, and as we prayed I wondered how this would work, since she had shown no interest in Jesus as the redeemer. It didn't matter a bit—I don't think the generous touch of Christ's love is limited to those who have the right theology. She didn't comment on any change to how she felt that day, but immediately after the prayer she was ready to work out the knots, and they moved on in their relationship.

If we are talking to a person of Muslim faith, they will usually agree that Jesus is the Prophet of healing. Explaining exactly how Jesus healed our brokenness may turn on the light for them to ask for the same and to find His healing for their own hurts. There may be a bigger disconnect in the area of "setting captives free" between the Muslim faith and ours, but a testimony from our own lives would probably be well received.

If you have never encountered the healing power of Jesus for yourself, but you are curious to learn more, I refer you to the work of Karl Lehman (a Christian psychiatrist) and Patty Velotta, found on the website immanuelpracticum.com. It was in this style of ministry that I initially found healing and freedom. My life has been enriched and reshaped over the past fifteen years through this kind of prayer.

I was recently at a memorial service for a woman who had lived her faith vibrantly into her late 80s. Printed on the back of the order of service for her memorial was this prayer that her children found in her Bible.

"Give me new experiences of Jesus each day, Father, so that my witness about Him may always be fresh, genuine, and attractive to a hopeless and superficial world."

It was evident in the memorial service that this dear friend had lived her life in the fresh presence of her Redeemer. She had touched the lives of many, many people right up to her last days—not with her rhetoric and theology but with an always vibrant love for each of those attending the service. Fresh awareness of Jesus is a powerful witness to His truth.

The second passage that I hold central to the sharing of faith is the beautiful verse about God becoming flesh so that we, in our finite understanding, would "behold" his glory. It wasn't about words and meanings and beliefs. We were invited to *behold*. And this is what Jesus did with his life—he gave out his identity in the perceptions of those who stopped to gaze…and get to know him, usually over time.

Jesus himself had very different ways of sharing his identity with almost everyone he met. Nothing in the Gospels would lead us to believe he had a four-step (or any other) program for leading everyone to the truth. The vast difference between his first encounter with the public and later encounters show that his approach was new each time. In Cana, he mysteriously turned the water into deluxe wine (food, again) inviting interest but answering no one's questions—not even his own mother's.

This is in contrast to an encounter with Zacchaeus—who was called to come down and serve him dinner (food again). And there was the encounter with Mary and Martha, each with their own questions and conversations with Jesus. Nothing was prepackaged, but a deep compassion for each one of the family sculpted a conversation uniquely designed for them. Jesus had an honest confrontation with Martha who needed prodding to go to the deeper levels of interest in what he was offering, getting her beyond the food.

When there was not yet enough interest in truth, Jesus used questions and often relied on a device—focusing on a mystery that needed to be unraveled, which was seen in so many of his parables. He rarely drew attention to himself, but was masterful at creating an interest in the deeper meaning behind what he said. That craving for deeper things led to the invitation he waited for—he wanted to be asked, invited to share his wisdom, teaching and healing power.

We were struck by the power of the invitation in our first six months in North Africa. We only lasted in the first country for that short sojourn, perhaps because we were a little too open with our witness of faith and the police got wind of this. We had been told to be very careful with how we shared, and in general we were. We waited to be asked about our faith more often than not. With most people this took time, but there was one unforgettable contrast.

In our first week there, the school where my husband worked hired a local teacher, Nasir, with impeccable English. Since there seemed to be a shortage of students (most classes had between three and six), I immediately suspected that Nasir was not actually hired to teach. It was my belief that he had been assigned to watch out for our every move and even assess why we were there.

This suspicion was confirmed, in my mind, as my husband and the other Canadian teacher, Dan, came home for lunch each day and told me about the questions Nasir was asking. He had numerous questions about our faith, most of them well-informed by the various schools of systematic theology. Neither my husband nor Dan shared my skepticism about Nasir, and they likely believed I was being a little paranoid. They continued to have lengthy discussions with him whenever he saw an opening and approached them.

One day I met Nasir for myself. He approached me while I was bringing my children in on a break to see their dad. I felt no need to continue the conversations that he had started with "the boys." But Nasir was insistent in asking and arguing about theological questions, so after a couple of minutes I said to him quite firmly, "I'll tell you what. Why don't we just jump to the end of this argument, and I'll agree that you win. You are obviously smarter than I am, so you are going to win in the end."

When Nasir continued to poke at me for answers, I told him that I would tell him one story before I left which, I announced, would be my answer to all the other questions. I told him a story I had read a few days previously in a book by Francis Frangipane (I don't recall which of his books it was in).

One day a master took his disciple to the lake with him. He had been teaching this disciple for some time, and the disciple thought he was doing quite well. The master took the disciple into the water and, expecting some great thing to happen, the disciple was very surprised when the master took a hold of his head and pushed it under the water. At first the disciple just wondered what the lesson was, but then he began to need some air, and still the master held him under. Then he began to thrash and try to get free as he realized his need was getting quite desperate, but the master refused to relinquish his hold. Finally the disciple realized that maybe this was the end, after all—for reasons he could not discern, the master had decided to take his life.

Just at that moment, the master let go, and the disciple came up out of the water gasping for breath, surprised, and more than slightly relieved.

When the disciple had recovered a little, he asked the master, "Why did you do that?"

To which the master replied, "When your desire for God is as great as the desire for oxygen you just experienced—then will you find Him."

I told Nasir quite boldly and bluntly that he should seek God and stop arguing theology. Then perhaps he would find his answers.

My husband and Dan continued to work with Nasir for several months. His determination to discuss every aspect of Christian "theory" never wavered, but he never showed any signs of being interested in a spiritual experience of his own. One day Nasir disappeared as quietly as he had appeared. Who knows what he had concluded about us—who knows if my story or the men's discussions had any impact on him. However, the story of the disciple gasping for air had impacted me deeply. It was analogous to my experience of living in a desert city with so few of the relationships that sustained me spiritually in my home setting. But compared to the local people, I still had a great deal of freedom.

We were aware that if the local people decided to become followers of Christ, they could face a death sentence. So we waited to be asked about our faith, and there were one or two opportunities that suggested there was interest. We spent much more time praying than we did talking about theology, and these were rich times of fellowship. Our understanding of God and grace grew in ways we had not fathomed.

My husband found a verse in John 17 that took on new meaning over these months. It turned out to be a powerful guide for how we lived our faith in this situation. In this chapter, Jesus is praying for His followers to know the rich love of the Father for them, which will then be expressed toward each other:

I am in them and you are in me, so that they may be made completely one, that the world may know you have sent me and have loved them as you have loved me. John 17:23

We talked about this verse and mulled over it in several of our prayer times. Like many scriptures, it seemed to take on a life of its own in this new context.

On the night before we were to leave, having been told that our visas had now expired, we invited all of the students onto our roof for a drink of soda pop, along with some brownies. This constituted a party—nothing like a sugar high to help say good-bye. The party was a fun way to end our time at the school, even though we were sad to leave. One of the students stayed a little longer, letting the others depart ahead of him. He wanted to speak with my husband privately.

He came with the longed for invitation. His heart was open and ready and curious. He wanted to hear about Jesus.

His questions were pointed and specific, and he asked for a copy of the Gospel—the *Injil*. The *Injil* is one of the holy books of Islam, though not all Muslims know this. There is a verse in the Qur'an that lists the holy books and the Gospel is included.

By asking for a copy of the *Injil*, this student was not actually breaking faith with his own religion. However, his request was prefaced with this explanation:

"You know, I have watched you and Dan very carefully because I wanted to find out if Christians were everything I had heard they were. I discovered that what I had been told is not true. Whenever I see you together, I see a kindness and respect between you that I have never seen before. Not once have I seen you speaking or treating each other in the way I expected Christians to behave. And because of the way you have shown respect and love for each other, I've come to believe that what you follow is the truth. Would it be possible for me to get a copy of the *Injil* (Gospel)?"

This student had seen exactly what my husband had understood from the verse in John 17— the love we have for each other is evidence of the truth: Jesus was sent by God as the true pathway to redemption and salvation.

The death and resurrection of Christ was not something we had talked about or explained to this student. It was something we had lived in the way we talked and worked and even in how we had "played" together. And through prayer—we had prayed together until we were a unified force—the light of God's presence had been seen through the relationships we had invested in. We had spoken the Gospel, but without the religious and theological words that so often consume our attention and build barriers to having faith in its inherent mystery.

The Gospel in its fullness is not something that can merely be put into a few phrases or explanations. We so often want to do that, but it is the whole of our lives that creates the "crate" that carries the glory of God. Redemption can only come in containers that have been cracked and broken—we know that part of the story well. We have to carry the glory within us in such a way that it is revealed through those cracks. It is not just what we talk about, though that is important. What we live in community creates the outline for others to begin to ask questions that will fill the gaps and draw them toward a relationship of their own with a God who longs to hear them say the words heard so often from Jesus,

"Our Father."

TIPS, SUGGESTIONS AND QUESTIONS:

Talking naturally about your faith—your thoughts and feelings about God is not easy for many people. If you want to be able to talk about your faith with people from other cultures, you probably need to be good at talking with people from your own background about your relationship with God. This would have to begin in relationships where you are safe to be vulnerable—friends or family. Where might you find people to talk with in this way?

Creating conversations that feel natural for talking about faith with people from other religious and cultural backgrounds are much more likely to be natural and welcomed if you show some curiosity and interest in what they believe and how they came to those beliefs. Don't just ask questions so you can get to the point where you can tell them what you think truth is. Ask and listen, be curious and try to understand—take time to learn.

QUESTIONS FOR REFLECTION:

Who are the people in your life who lived out their faith in such a way that you wanted to learn more or take part in their community? What were their personal characteristics that attracted you to their belief or value system? What characteristics would you most like to have in your own life that would create a desire in others to learn more about you, your value system and your faith?

~ 15 ~

Ashes and Roses

Beauty surrounds us, but usually we need to be walking in a garden to know it.

Rumi

When we first arrived in North Africa, we had a second floor apartment with access to the roof. If we wanted to enjoy being outdoors, we could go up to the roof with its high walls—so high we could not be seen by neighbours on their roofs. Privacy concerns trumped the view of the single palm tree out on the sandy desert—which was what I could see when I succumbed to my own curiosity and dragged a chair up to look over the wall.

The children played on our rooftop, we ate our supper up there in better weather, and on winter mornings we could warm our stiff limbs in the sun. The roof also held the line where I would hang our clothes to dry. When summer came, I could hang the clothes up along my 30 foot line and then go back to the starting point and take them all back down—that's how long it takes for summer fabrics to dry in 45C heat, even without a breeze!

I noticed a verse in Isaiah soon after we arrived. Many portions of Scripture had come alive in these months of living in an isolated city surrounded by the Sahara. But one verse in chapter 35 seemed to be more than just renewed by the pertinence of this context. It spoke of roses blooming in the desert and seemed to have a "vibe"—a sense that this was God's truth to my life. It was a promise pertinent to the part of the world where I was living, loving, and praying.

Our landlord who lived below us on the ground floor had studied in Canada for a few years. His front yard was distinctive for the beautiful mass of daisies and carnations growing there—thriving even in the cool nights of winter, though not doing so well when "spring" came. Spring was two weeks long, a combination of moderate nights that were not as cold as winter, and then daytime temperatures that soared abruptly and beyond reason. Mid-morning each day, the scorching air of 40C started to hit us like hot bricks, hard and fast. Another few weeks and we were stretching our survival skills to find our way through nights too hot to sleep and days that were at least 45C.

Amazingly, there were a couple of rose bushes in the landlord's garden, almost lost in the lavish sprays of daisies and carnations. I thought it was a miracle that they were still alive in the extreme heat that came so suddenly.

On Fridays we would go out with a student and visit one of the farms that surrounded our city, another exhibit of verdant beauty. It seemed that every family had a farm where root vegetables grew abundantly in the sandy soil. Each student would walk us through their fields and tell us about each crop, not realizing that we had been on an identical tour of a twin farm the week before with another student. We took great notice of the wells, intrigued by the power they held—it seemed incongruous to see the disparity between the land that was irrigated and the land that was not. The greenery of carrot tops, beet greens, and potato plants stopped abruptly where the water stopped and the sand began.

One of the farms was run by a student's uncle, who lived in a small house on the property. He was excited to show us his pride and joy, a large rose bush the size of a tree, with beautiful pink blooms. Around the back of his house, in an area chosen for ideal shade, he had two rows of rose cuttings, arranged in the sand. The key to getting the cuttings to develop roots was to cut them before the weather got too hot, but at the exact time that they were starting to sprout new branches in the turning weather at winter's end.

The loose sandy soil—if you can call it soil—was an ideal place for roots to begin to grow. There was less resistance to new growth in sand. Here, in this sandy garden, I saw that if water is plentiful and runs over the roots, not sitting "soggy" around them, rose bushes love the heat. I didn't realize how important this was until a few years and a few lost rose bushes later.

I didn't know much about gardens in the desert, so I was amazed at the sight of these roses beginning to bloom in the desert heat—and on the night we visited this farm, the verse from Isaiah 35 came alive—as vibrant as the pink rose the farm uncle had given me to bring home.

The wilderness and the dry land shall be gladdened; and the desert shall rejoice, and blossom as the rose. Isaiah 35:1

I knew just how gladdened that land could be. After months away from the green land we called "home," the rose the farmer gave me was a precious item, a treasured gift! We'd made it through Valentine's Day and a birthday without the sighting of a flower shop, though we had our landlord's garden to walk past each day. But this rose had the special meaning imposed on it by the promise of Isaiah.

When we moved to another city in the neighbouring country, I kept this verse as a promise that infused my prayers with hope. I came to believe that my purpose in being in this desert was to pray this verse into reality.

I found rose bushes being sold at the old city gates and brought a couple of them home to the small patches of dirt in my tiled front yard. Not understanding that the heavy soil with poor drainage was the opposite of what roses needed, I found them difficult to grow.

Then on the weekend of the Big Feast when the neighbour kids brought a live sheep home from the market in preparation for the family banquet, my roses became a fast food stop for the animal. Roses don't survive when every single leaf is munched off and the stems are chewed down to the ground. At least these ones did not.

If my roses had been a glorious thriving delight of colour and beauty, I would have cried when the sheep ate them. But I was just mad at the boys who generously opened our gate and hosted a rosebush dinner for their sheep while I was out. Roses from scripture were fine, but real roses, in my garden, felt like a symbol of hopelessness.

It was another five years before I planted roses again.

In the meantime, this verse with the symbolism of roses blooming in the desert was a strong theme in my prayer life. I remained steadfast in my conviction that this desert place, as spiritually arid as the moon's surface, would someday sprout with new life. But I didn't think this was a literal, physical promise.

I don't know why I changed my mind about planting roses—I think it was the pure temptation of the sight of rose bushes I found on a visit to France. They were sold in "safe" wrappings—the branches covered in wax and the roots carefully ensconced in burlap bags of rich loam. We traveled home on the ferry toting five healthy rose cuttings with us.

They didn't thrive, but these roses did well enough to convince me to try some local bushes once again. And this time I launched a garden of roses successfully, possibly with some strong support from the worm family I had been feeding with onion and carrot tops!

Six weeks after I planted the first locally purchased rose bush, I counted the buds and blossoms. Sixty! Sixty buds coming into bloom all on a bush I had planted in mid-February—about forty-five days before I counted them. I know that because I planted the rose bush a few days before we started a season of praise. We had set aside forty days for a prayer journey of praise and worship. We had asked God for nothing during that time and had spent hours each morning in worship in our home. I counted the buds on our last day.

This bush was a vibrant coral colour—chosen because that was what was available at the only nursery I could find on a trip to the capital city. The buds were tiny but intense in colour—and they brought as much joy as a garden can give.

God spoke to me over and over in that garden. When I weeded, I prayed—for people we knew in the city. When I watered, I prayed—for colleagues and family. When we got a farm truck to bring manure, I prayed—not sure what to pray about, I listened for God to speak. I started to realize that there was some significance to putting the waste of life into the land so that it would contribute to the well-being of what was growing. The idea that my brokenness could be redeemed to give life to something new began a journey in my soul, there in my rose garden.

In the meantime, we had also contracted someone to dig us a well, and the abundance of water meant we had one of the nicest gardens in our neighbourhood. People we didn't know would comment that they loved to peer through the gate. Friends coming from another city would walk in and say, "I've been looking forward to the green in your garden all day. It is so restful." I began to understand it was part of the promise I had been praying for. There was a visibility to this garden that was just as spiritual as the prayers I had been uttering for nearly ten years.

I finally got the full measure of the meaning of this after another seven years of gardening. On this day, I was praying with a friend, and in my front hallway there was a vase filled with the giant rose blooms from the rose "tree" that had taken over one end of the garden. In the intervening years, three of my bushes had grown magnificently. There were seasons when I could pick 40 rose blossoms over the course of a week—filling each room with a bouquet and giving some away.

My friend Sue was sitting in our front room with me where we had a habit of taking times of long silence in God's presence. Neither of us felt the need to say anything in these times, but we came away with a deep sense of God-with-us. Sometimes there were things to share after our silence, but we didn't pray with that expectation. It was the presence itself that delighted us—a value and joy that we shared.

As we prayed on this day, I decided I needed to use the bathroom. I walked across the front hallway and, seeing the rose bouquet there, I began to consider the verse about beauty for ashes. By the time I got back to our quiet front room, I was convinced that God was speaking to me about our city—that the rose garden I had grown with sweet fragrant blooms was a picture of the plans He had for a city that was steeped in centuries of violence and despair. This city was considered the suicide capital of our nation.

As I sat a little longer with Sue, still in silence, I began to feel that this was not just a thought about ashes and beauty. I became convinced that I was supposed to do something with this prayer. There was a large lot next to my house where people threw branches they pruned from bougainvillea vines. The branches were spiny with thorns but eventually someone would come and cut them up for firewood. More was delivered than taken away on any given day.

I decided that what was stirring in my spirit, in the form of a prayer, was a practical, physical need to gather some thorny branches and burn them. These ashes could then be put on my rose bushes, symbolically, so they would turn to beauty in good season.

Until I told this plan to Sue at the end of our prayer time, I had no idea that ashes are actually good fertilizer. They work as if the decomposition process has been accelerated, and the nutrients are delivered into the soil through the ash.

Sue had lived in another African nation and had participated in renewing soil this way. She informed me that this was a good idea on every level—spiritual and physical.

And so a few weeks later, seven of us gathered up some branches, dragging them home to a giant bonfire one week before Good Friday, at the beginning of the week of Passion. On Good Friday at sunset we put the ashes on the plants and left it to penetrate the soil. We celebrated Easter in the hope and joy that a tangible act like this would bring a visible result in the rose bushes themselves.

Over the next six months we watched the roses flourish with renewed vigour. As that happened, God stirred reflections within me about prayer—the burning and the delivery of ashes. I had lived in prayer for many years—I had embraced a journey of faith that was preached so often without words. But this act, the burning of thorny branches and the feeding of rose trees with ashes, this was the "act of prayer" that convinced me—life is prayer. Every step we take, every hand we hold, every hug we give, these are all prayers when the presence of Christ is in them—in us, as we deliver them.

Prayer is more than the words we say when we talk with God. It goes beyond the utterances that we are conscious of—sometimes we stand in a gap in silence and the prayers are in our feet, staying in the place where nothing exists. Not yet.

Jesus gave a prayer to His disciples—turning them to face God as their Father and as the Holy sovereign power. The third phrase in this prayer is, "Your will be done, on earth as it is in heaven."

My actionable prayer of ash as rose food was just this: doing the will of God, opening heaven's window to see what He wanted done, and then being the hands that pulled thorny branches to our fire and poured out ash on the soil.

I needed to be ready to pray for friends and neighbours when they were in distress. I needed to explain my love of God when I met someone who was seeking spiritual reality. I needed to be prepared to open the door for those who wanted to know about Jesus.

But I needed to live the way my garden lives: in every season putting down deeper roots or pushing up new branches with opening buds. It was my very breath and life that was given out of God's glory that I was living to bring glory back to Him—and in these seasons, His presence was evidenced in my soul. The Gospel was growing *in me.*

Friendships grow much like gardens do. They need the seeds to be planted and for the sun to shine and the soil to give nutrients. And then they need time. Time is an essential element for growing things.

Sometimes new leaves unfold, and we are not even sure what this plant is going to be. We think it might be a melon, and it turns out we are growing a pumpkin—that happened to me. A plant "volunteered" from my composting hole one year, and I knew by the leaves it would be from the squash or melon family. Then the flowers opened—golden yellow. I peered at them, thinking they might be cucumber blossoms or maybe melon. When the fruit appeared, it looked like zucchini—not my favourite, but at least we had a product. As it grew, the kids and I became sure it was not zucchini, but we still puzzled over what it could be. For a while we thought it must be a watermelon; it was a daily guessing game. Finally our belief that it was a squash was confirmed, but only when we brought it in to the cutting board and opened it.

Some of my kids were sad that it was only a squash, something like a pumpkin but with the shape of a watermelon. We'd never seen a vegetable exactly like this before, and we never saw another one. But I can still taste it as I write this—it made the most delicious soup and a casserole of sweet mash for our Christmas dinner that year.

This is a picture of our lives as well. So often we don't actually know what the fruit is going to be. We have choices to make about what seeds we are going to plant and where and how many. Sometimes something "volunteers" that we didn't realize we had planted. But the garden is ours to tend.

We have the ability to create conditions that will encourage growth. We keep the weeds under control so the nutrients will nourish the seeds. But often we are not sure exactly what the outcome is going to be—we live in faith that there is Life.

The seeds are the Gospel, not just words that explain the Gospel, but active lives that live the truth of our redemptive gift and give grace generously. Living the Gospel is less complicated but more complex than words can contain—it pulls us back to the perfect relationship of love that we were offered as humans in the garden of Eden.

The faith we have is that God's love is a sovereign, perfect reality, as personal as it is mysterious. The conditions we are responsible for are the investment of our time and effort—our loyalty to a God who lives within us, and to the friends we have chosen to walk beside. Our prayers attend to the atmosphere around the seeds we plant each day by living in peace, hope, justice and love.

And the rest, the mystery of unfolding a human heart to the Light of Truth, that is the work of God, who is ever calling His creation to come to Him. We participate, but He is the sun that shines and gives light and the rain that falls and waters the growth. He decides the seasons, and in His time there is the fruit of redemption.

TIPS, SUGGESTIONS AND QUESTIONS:

There will always be things in our lives that are hard—things that we need to allow time to change before they become a "useful" part of our lives—like thorn bushes being burned and ashes feeding the soil. Quite often the process is hard to recognize while we are in it.

Sharing hard stories is one of the best ways to find healing for the deep hurts that have scarred our hearts. When those losses and hurts have happened in traumatic ways, the instincts we have to shut down our emotions are actually saving us from being crushed by the pain.

Many of the refugees and immigrants that are coming to North America have experienced the kind of loss and trauma that was too much to deal with in the circumstances of their life. They may look, sound, or behave like someone who has enclosed the hurt behind a wall of hardness. It may take a while for them to believe that your friendship is genuine, and it *should* take a while for them to disclose these hard stories to you. Human instincts are there to shield us from too much hurt.

But letting people who have experienced loss tell their story in a warm, inviting friendship that offers understanding and affirmation is possibly the most treasured gift we can give. Don't take this gift lightly. If they start to share and we decide the friendship is too much for us, there is a risk they will experience rejection on top of the great pain of losses. We may think a counsellor would be a better place for them to find healing, but our genuine friendship and love is potentially even more healing than a trained counsellor. Our love can be real, and real love is what every counsellor will acknowledge is the first need that humans must have in order to flourish.

QUESTIONS FOR REFLECTION:

In what ways do you see your life like a garden? If this analogy is not something you can see in your own life, how would you see your life as something that you attend to in order to make sure there is healthy growth? Who are the people who taught you to be good at attending to growth? How do you want to be like them for others—family, friends and those you work alongside?

~ 16 ~

Foreigner Among Friends

Only those who will risk going too far
can possibly find out how far one can go.
T.S. Eliot

The heritage of our faith begins with the story of a journey. In Abraham's day, such a journey was a one-way ticket—he left his father's home for another country, and there was no question that this was forever, for good. His journey took him about 1100 miles, not far in today's world of rapid travel—but for Abraham it was a lifetime of new experiences.

Additionally, Abraham's family—Isaac (and Ishmael), Jacob, Esau, and their families— encountered the challenges of cross cultural living. This theme continued through many Old Testament stories of faith, for example Moses, Joshua, and Daniel, along with many others. Ruth and Esther are remarkable women living in cross-cultural scenarios, adapting and making an impact of enduring importance. We have a strong heritage of the message that our faith is for all nations—Abraham was instructed from the beginning:

Go out from your land,
your relatives,
and your father's house
to the land that I will show you.

I will make you into a great nation,
I will bless you,
I will make your name great,
and you will be a blessing.

I will bless those who bless you,
I will curse anyone who treats you with contempt,
and all the peoples on earth
will be blessed through you. Genesis 12:1-3 CSB

Henri Nouwen says that we are all sojourners on a pilgrimage of faith. Our lives, whether they take us far from home or not, are a journey.[12] Often it is the unknown that gets us to the destination that God has for our soul. Discomfort can be a great teacher, but finding our true "home" is the journey that we all pursue.

My parents came from countries on two different continents. Before my third birthday, our family settled into our third country, on a third continent. If life is a pilgrimage, my journey began before I could even walk. The likelihood of transition was consistently before me, and I took for granted that the adage, "there's no place like home" didn't mean a physical house—it meant a permanent connection to my family. It was a moveable tryst of care, provision, safety, and connection that followed us across the world—wherever we were together, I was "home."

Our long summer break came over the Christmas holidays to suit our South American seasons. Other families made exciting trips to places like Macchu Picchu and Iguazu Falls. Our vacations served a dual purpose.

My dad's little Cessna benefited from a maintenance visit to an aviation base set in a clearing beside a tropical lake about four hours away. The village was a string of houses settled along the road running from the airplane hangars to a school for the families who lived there. This was our usual vacation destination.

One day as we walked from the hangar toward the lake where we planned to spend the morning, my mom sang a hymn I had never heard before. She sang hymns often, but these new words had me thinking.

---

[12] Henri J.M. Nouwen, The Way of the Heart (New York: Ballantine Books, 1981).

It was a song about heaven, sung wistfully, as by one who longed to be there now. It referred to heaven as "home"—so distant from what I felt about home and my adventurous family. We sang a chorus at school with similar words, but I had never stopped to think about them:

This world is not my home I'm just a passing through
My treasures are laid up somewhere beyond the blue
The angels beckon me from heaven's open door
And I can't feel at home in this world anymore.[13]

I felt genuinely worried—would she prefer to leave for heaven? It disturbed me a little that she would sing this. I was facing immortality and eternity for the first time with thoughtful consideration.

Our subsequent discussion quelled my fears. Mom explained that we aren't actually supposed to feel that this world is our home. We have another home, one that is more complete and satisfying, and we yearn for that place—this was her understanding of Scripture. She managed to explain this in a way that my 10-year-old mind could almost grasp.

Hebrews 11 talks about Abraham's journey, which took him far from his family. This journey set a context for Abraham's mindset of seeing that there was a greater "city"—a place ahead for him, beyond this world.

For he (Abraham) was looking forward to the city that has foundations, whose architect and builder is God. Hebrews 11:10 CSB

James expands on this:

For we do not have an enduring city here; instead, we seek the one to come. James 1:14 CSB

The theme of roving citizenship, of moving across cultures and nations, is rooted in Biblical stories. In the story of the Babylonian exile the people of Israel are removed from the home they built with so much determination. Now they find themselves among foreigners. Again.

Jeremiah gives the Israelites instructions to make themselves "at home"—this will not be a short exile. Jeremiah's prophecy echoes instructions in Deuteronomy given to the people of Israel when they were leaving slavery and creating their homeland—the "Promised

---

[13] *Albert E. Brumley, Acclaim Music, 1952,*
http://www.metrolyrics.com/this-world-is-not-my-home-lyrics-hank-thompson.html

Land." They should build houses, plant gardens, and celebrate weddings, presumably followed by children. These three activities represent the survival of humans; we must feed ourselves, find protective shelter, and reproduce. These three also constitute the basics of life that bind families together with purpose. In a foreign place, the people God has chosen to reveal His plans are told to "settle in"—to become a part of the fabric of the world around them.

Build houses and live in them. Plant gardens and eat their produce. Find wives for yourselves, and have sons and daughters. Find wives for your sons and give your daughters to men in marriage so that they may bear sons and daughters. Multiply there; do not decrease. Pursue the well-being of the city I have deported you to. Pray to the Lord on its behalf, for when it thrives, you will thrive. Jeremiah 29: 5-7 CSB

Jeremiah's message was, "God is with you in this upheaval,"—this cross-cultural shift is a part of His bigger purpose.

The people of Israel saw themselves as ones who lived in the space "between." There was the fallen, broken world all around. And there was the glorious, restored world of the afterlife. For the present, their purpose was to live in the space between, keeping the redemptive presence and purposes of God in their homes through the rituals of their faith. In Christ, these redemptive purposes become clearer, but they influenced the lives of the Old Testament characters.[14] The visual of God's redemptive purposes was to serve across nations, not just for the one "chosen" group.

The writers of Hebrews and James talked about the yearning that we have for the next world. This was the worldview the Israelites carried with them. It is what we all carry inside—a longing for a space called "home," a place where we are protected, provided for, and understood. Not a house, but a relational structure that feels secure and predicts a good future. God with us is our "home."

How then do we live in the between in today's world? This question is part of the pilgrimage of life. How do we do this when we have crossed the world, or just crossed the street to meet across cultures? How do we bring the message of "home" with us? The message is that there is One who protects, provides and sees into our souls to cherish and understand us.

The promise made to Abraham goes beyond our own nation and culture. He was blessed by God in order to be a blessing to all nations.

---

[14]*Jeremy Duncan, "Exemptions from War," Sermon Series: Our Next Steps, Part 2" September 17, 2017, https://www.youtube.com/watch?v=2faR0QLNBOI.*

Paul pulls this forward in the epistles when he talks about reaching across all nations.

So then you are no longer foreigners and strangers, but fellow citizens with the saints, and members of God's household, built on the foundation of the apostles and prophets, with Christ Jesus himself as the cornerstone. In him the whole building, being put together, grows into a holy temple in the Lord. In him you are also being built together for God's dwelling in the Spirit. Ephesians 2:19-22 CSB

And again,

This grace was given to me—the least of all the saints—to proclaim to the Gentiles the incalculable riches of Christ, and to shed light for all about the administration of the mystery hidden for ages in God who created all things. This is so that God's multi-faceted wisdom may now be made known through the church to the rulers and authorities in the heavens. This is according to his eternal purpose accomplished in Christ Jesus our Lord. Ephesians 3:8-11 CSB

This thought is echoed in the poetry of Revelation where we read about all nations, all cultures, gathering before the throne of God, worshiping Jesus as the Redeemer.

And they sang a new song:
You are worthy to take the scroll
and to open its seals,
because you were slaughtered,
and you purchased people
for God by your blood
from every tribe and language
and people and nation.
You made them a kingdom
and priests to our God,
and they will reign on the earth. Revelation 5:9-10

Together, the nations are creating the "household of God"—that home we are all yearning for. In the meantime, we live the Gospel of redemption in the "between."

When we moved to our third house in North Africa, I read the passage in Jeremiah as relevant to my connection to the city we lived in. I had never lived in a house for more than 4 years so planting trees seemed too long term for me.

We found a house which had a safe space for our children to play. There was also a hole in the cement filled with dirt and dry weeds. The weed garden was a bonus for my benefit. That garden became my metaphor for thriving in the desert.

We paid for two trucks of sheep manure and uprooted the acre of weeds that had wedged their way in. I tried out different varieties of flowering shrubs. The tree with purple blooms hanging in clusters gave delicate beauty. The tall slim tree with yellow trumpet flowers grew from four feet to 20 each year and gave shade to carnations, daisies, verbena, and geraniums. When we left for a few weeks of summer, I hoped the little ones would survive the heat. They rarely did, and I would come home to replant them, determined to beat the desert. Gradually we filled the garden with hardier plants.

It was a complete surprise to me that roses were just as sturdy as the yellow trumpet tree and the blue pinwheel flower that survived summer. After five years I found another lady with a garden. When I asked who took care of it when she travelled, she looked at me aghast. "When I go away? I don't go away! I can't leave my garden, it would die."

"You don't leave, not even for a day?" I asked, wondering how she survived the heat!

"No, I don't even go to the beach for a day," was her passionate reply. I understood her dedication, and I recognized that my own did not match up. When you want to grow a garden in the desert, your determination has to match the challenge. Her garden featured exquisite and exotic blooms—I was happy with my verbena and honeysuckle, both survivors.

I settled into my neighbourhood and adapted to the weather. I met my neighbours and learned to build friendships that satisfied me. My children found friends and were doing well. Our family was living in the "between." Perhaps most meaningful were the times we were "neighbours," called on for support in times of genuine need. I was learning to live the Gospel—it was not always easy, but I was gaining understanding.

The Gospels, which relay the narrative of Jesus life, are not short on stories of cross cultural encounters. Jesus said many provocative things—some to people of other cultures, but many to his own countrymen. Among them is his reply when he said, "Love your neighbour," and was asked, "Who is my neighbour?"

Jesus told the story of a traveller battered nearly to death by thieves, left to die beside the road. It was the road "in between." The story pointedly referred to the choices made by the religious and judicial leaders of the day—avoiding contact. Then a man of the most despised nationality came by and acted with nobility, caring for the struggling traveller. At his own expense, this foreigner made sure the traveller's needs were met—

he didn't stop his own life to do this, but he made sure the job was done well.

The advantage of the world we live in is that we no longer need to travel to experience new adventures. The cultures of nearly every continent are nearby, often on our own street. The friendships we pursue with people of different backgrounds will take us on the spiritual pilgrimage that Henri Nouwen talks about. It's a journey that will challenge us to see the world differently, accept with grace the changes we are invited to embrace, and deeply reflect on who we are as a people of redemption.

But we are left with the strong message in the story Jesus told. If we fight for justice or preach religion without stopping to help other travellers who have experienced loss and hardship, we are not living out the second of the great commandments—to love others.

When we are good neighbours, we inevitably create the signposts that signal the way "home"—to the One who provides and redeems. And He fills the longings within us. We are part of His plan to care for the battered travellers in this space in between.

TIPS, SUGGESTIONS AND QUESTIONS:

When we leave our homeland, our culture, and all that is familiar behind, we inevitably move into a space that feels insecure and difficult. But we also turn a page—open a door. The uncertainty we find in that gap discloses an opportunity for insight and understanding that we won't gain by staying in the safety of the status quo. In this place of unfamiliarity, we begin to sift through what we need to keep and what we perhaps need to discard. We question our values and priorities in the light of a culture that holds other things as immovable or even sacred. And this, for a person of faith, is always a good thing. This is where we grow.

We live in a world where the idea of making an 1100 kilometre journey without planning ahead would make most of us crazy. But life without plans is normal for many places in the world. When we first moved to North Africa we frequently heard, "It's better to not make plans. Things go better if you don't plan." We thought it was hilarious that two years later a group of students who debriefed with us would think that saying was strange and crazy. We'd come to see there was truth in it.

Can you list some things that will go better without plans? Can you imagine how your friendships might grow if you didn't make plans—what would need to be in place? How about your relationship with God, might that be enhanced by avoiding planning ahead? Can you even imagine it?

When you build a friendship with people from traditional cultures, you need to be ready for some unplanned and unexpected events. Being flexible is important. If you can imagine how you might grow from this even if you find yourself frustrated in the middle of something, it will help you to stay positive and embrace the opportunities.

One specific way that we exhibit this difference is that we rarely or never show up uninvited at friends' houses. Try this (when you are ready for the excitement) with a friend from another background—just to check out what might happen or grow from the experience.

QUESTIONS FOR REFLECTION:

One of the things that planning does is give us the illusion of control. Most of us take a good look at our lives at some point to see if we might be ever-so-slightly a control freak. The things we try to control are often our blindspots—things we, by nature, cannot see unless someone points them out for us. Getting involved in another culture is one way of starting to see those places, through another lens. Are you ready for this?

Appendix

Desert Prayers

In my first year of college I discovered the writings of the "Desert Fathers." Most of them were monks who had devoted their life to prayer. Many had spent months or years in the isolation of deserted places and their views on theology and prayer stemmed from times when they spoke only with God, intimately, for days on end. Their writings appealed to me. And they contrasted sharply with the Christianity I was familiar with.

When I was growing up, prayer was modelled as a stylized monologue with God on the listening end. Adults gave Him their best advice and then listed off the actions that would serve His best interests. The really great leaders prayed as if they were the presidential advisors with expertise required by a powerful God that didn't quite have the knowledge base to match His sovereignty.

We pray. God moves. Things change; people change.

We tend to think that our prayers should change *other* people.

I found out how poorly this worked when my mom got sick and we all prayed for her to be healed. After she died, I felt I had a choice to be angry at God or to blame her death on evil. It seemed obvious to me that I should not blame God. But this decision left my paradigm of prayer in chaos.

The writings of the Desert Fathers, the "mystics" as they were called, had a profound impact on my search for a relationship with God that made sense in the trauma of this loss. These writers viewed a conversation with God in a very different way than the evangelical Christian tradition. To them prayer was a dialogue in which the Divine spoke up for Himself. And sometimes He chose silence—which was not without meaning. According to the mystics, we were not expected to always understand—this was affirming to my own journey with God. He had remained silent, and I did not understand.

There was plenty of space in the theology of the Desert Fathers for the mystery of God. For the first time I articulated the decision that had carried me through the loss of my mother—it didn't have to make sense. God was a mystery. I could not ever, in my finite mind, understand fully the expanse of His character, His ways. Almost certainly I would never grasp the bigger picture of how life and death served His purposes for the here and now, or for time-eternal yet to come for us.

With a hungry soul, I delved into the new perspective on God that these writers described. Each book by these "mystics" carried a different facet of this new way of seeing God.

One of my friends explained the Russian mystics to me, sharing his enthusiasm for the inspiration they gave him. These men didn't go to the desert to get away from people—sometimes it was quite the opposite. They went there because the solitude pushed them to face what was inside their own souls. And when that had happened, they were prepared to help others.

The desert-dwelling monks stayed in the solitude of the wilderness and waited for those who wanted their counsel to come and find them. The act of going on a pilgrimage to the house of a spiritual hermit, taking time away to focus on what God might be saying, was a crucial part of what these spiritual Fathers and counsellors offered.

I was willing to go on that journey into the desert to discover God. I just didn't realize it would be a journey that would take nearly thirty years. I didn't even notice that this journey was literally into the Sahara until I looked back in retrospect—with the proverbial 20/20 vision of hindsight.

In that first year of reading the Desert Fathers, I learned that prayer is supposed to change *me*, not the circumstances or people that surround me. And that change would be generated not so much out of my own effort but by the constant, life-giving presence of God around and in me. I was not necessarily tuned in to this presence, but with or without my noticing, God was always a part of my life.

The Desert Fathers taught me to pay attention to this consuming truth. They called me to tune in to the utterly astounding gift of being in the Father's "eyes." Not just sometimes, but all the time.

I first learned to pay attention to this as a "breath prayer"—a phrase you practice as you breathe in and out. This kind of prayer is a habit cultivated so that as surely as we breathe throughout the day, we can also maintain an awareness of God with us. We develop inner focus on

God's presence as well as dependence on His goodness to sustain us as we pair breathing with prayer.

There, into these new thoughts, I learned a prayer that set me up for inner growth with both freedom and humility. My job was to pray this as a rhythm of life, breathing in on the first phrase and out on the second phrase—praying it as often as I could remember throughout each day. The first breath prayer I learned was called the "Sinner's Prayer," familiar from the gospel story in Luke 18, though this was a common phrase in many requests made of Jesus.

"*Lord Jesus Christ, have mercy on me, a sinner.*"

Prayer that begins with a confession of my own shortcomings and needs, creates a wide space for the grace of God to take root and flourish in me. Here on the fringe of the Sahara, this prayer I had learned from the Desert Fathers continued to help me grow into myself, often with a greater understanding of where my own culture could be disregarded but my identity—my self—didn't need to be discarded. And I could approach people of a different culture with that same measure of grace.

There was an effect on how I lived out my relationships with people around me. It pushed me to approach people who are different than myself—visibly, or invisibly, slightly or vastly—with a margin for discovery. This humble expectation to learn started to replace the defensive stance that is so tempting to our human perspective.

My time living in a desert city of North Africa pushed me to pray with greater desire for the grace and mercy of God to fill my soul. My prayers went a lot like this:

"Lord Jesus, have mercy on me, a sinner. Fill me with Your grace and lead me into deeper understanding of what it means that each human being is formed in Your image and as such bears Your glory. We are all equally Yours and equally broken. Fill me with grace and may I, by Your redemption, bear Your glory and shine the light of the Gospel on others today. I ask that this prayer would be lifted and given life by the breath of Your Holy Spirit in me."

As my years in the Sahara went on, I became more familiar with the writing and traditions of Ignatius of Loyola. These drew me to another Scripture passage that furthered my journey. This turned me toward a prayer that is born of the realization that any devotion I have for God comes from God's love for me. It comes from a very simple statement made by the "disciple whom Jesus loved."

We love because He first loved us. 1 John 4:19.

I had a tradition of good works driving my faith during my years leading up to the discovery of this jewel from Ignatian spirituality. Even though I didn't agree with the idea of earning God's favour, I had slipped into a mentality of works, trying harder—ever harder, and yet even harder— to prove my love for God and to grow my own love for Him into maturity. It was an exhausting effort.

Faith is much simpler than that. He who loved us perfectly from the moment of our conception is willing to fill us with His love. *When we are well loved, we love well.* But first we must be filled.

When I stopped trying hard to love God perfectly and started joyfully receiving His love, my heart softened and changed. I was living in a city where people were not generally soft hearted toward each other, and my reaction to some of what happened was to grit my teeth and through my clenched jaw pray (not necessarily aloud), "God, You can bless them. You told us to bless our enemies, so bless them."

Then one year as I contemplated and asked God what he wanted me to change in the new year (a form of a New Year's resolution), I came to an idea which resonated as the answer to that prayer. I decided to use the first ten minutes of each day in a new way. No longer would I lie there pushing myself to get out of bed and face the day—truthfully it took me about ten minutes to muster the energy to get going. Instead, I would spend ten minutes reflecting on and inviting God's love for me to settle deeper into my spirit and soul—to fill me. I would stop trying so hard and start receiving. I would start each day with a full tank of love—I resolved to 'indulge' in this prayer until I *felt* loved. It was more than just a cognitive activity.

This was such a great "spiritual exercise" that at the end of the year I decided to keep it as a permanent fixture in my walk with God. As a prayer, it went something like this:

"Thank you, Father, for the deep, pure, unfailing love You have for me. I am barely able to understand it, but I open myself up to receive it. Open my eyes to see all the ways You are showing me Your love throughout this day. Give me the grace to let my heart rest in Your love and grow softer toward You."

This may sound like a prayer that is mainly for your own benefit, but it is impossible to be filled with God's love and have that tender gift touch your own soul without the overflow affecting those around you.

The third prayer is one that comes from my favourite Scripture about Jesus. But it does a full circle and takes me back to one of the first things that changed my thinking from the writings of the mystics in my first year of college. It starts with the description written by John, the beloved disciple, in the first chapter of his Gospel—

The Word took on flesh and became human and chose to live alongside us. We have seen Him, enveloped in undeniable splendour—the one true Son of the Father—evidenced in the perfect balance of grace and truth. John 1:14

This verse speaks of the Glory of God—the very central identity of God: *kabod*. By sending Christ to live among us, God revealed His full glory to us.

The mystics had taught me something that had changed my perspective on myself. Like Jesus, I was created to bear a unique expression of God's image, and thus His glory. Albeit marred and broken, there is something in me that is an essential part of the reflection of God—and it is unique to me. My walk with God, should move me toward a more perfect version of His image, but it has been there all along.

We are inadequate, cracked reflections of God—falling short of that glory. Perhaps humans were initially made to live out *all* of that glory, but instead we stumble through life, less than what we were made for. Still, each one of us bears the image of God, and the potential to reveal His glory resides within us.

This idea was a contrast to how I had been taught to think of myself. My upbringing had hammered into me that my identity was something marred and degenerate. I had never felt that anything in me was good or glorious or based in Light. I needed to be replaced with only Jesus—but it was not clear to me how to do that, so naturally it would be a struggle. This new way of seeing myself was astonishing. Refreshing.

Now I was free to grow into my own self—to believe what Psalm 139 said about God's creative touch on my life before I was born. I was allowed to be pleased with things I was good at—to rejoice in the ways I could offer my abilities or strengths in the service of God's kingdom. Not everything about me needed to beaten down. In fact, the words of Psalm 139 suggested that in some ways, the work of God in forming me was "wondrous." This was a far cry from what I heard during my years of growing up.

For it was you who created my inward parts;
you knit me together in my mother's womb.
I will praise you
because I have been remarkably and wondrously made.
Your works are wondrous,
and I know this very well.
My bones were not hidden from you
when I was made in secret,
when I was formed in the depths of the earth.
Your eyes saw me when I was formless;
all my days were written in your book and planned
before a single one of them began.
God, how precious your thoughts are to me;
how vast their sum is! Psalm 52

From the desert fathers, I learned to create room in myself to grow into this revised identity. The prayer for mercy had started me down this path. Instead of leading me to arrogance and pride about how great I am because I reflect the image of God, this prayer led me to a sense of how far I was from that image being fully formed in me. I needed the mercy of God, the generosity of His grace for me. Even though I don't deserve it, God gave himself so I could live in the full capacity of who I was created to be.

The desert fathers had sprinkled seeds generously into the theology of my identity. They had sown the idea that my spiritual journey should take me ever closer to the way God made me distinctly and uniquely me. His image was deliberately placed into my soul, my personality, my inner self. By running away from who God made me to be, I was not becoming more godly and godlike, but less so.

By being fully myself, true to myself, I was honouring God's creation—of me. And in doing so, I was a picture of God's *kabod*—His glory. To myself, but also to others. The prayer from John 1:14 took me further in this journey of identity.

By logic, however, this impacted immensely the attitude with which I approached others. If this was true for me it meant that everyone else also carried the image of God, the light of God within their soul. My respect for how they reveal God opens me to a relationship where I am tempted to look for this, not negate it or destroy it in any way. I found it hard in my human limitations to live this out fully—but it became an important part of how I viewed humanity, myself included.

This prayer, less obvious and more challenging, embraces the potential in my own soul to reveal the Glory of God through who I am.

"Father, thank You for sending Jesus as the perfect picture of Your Glory, to dwell here on earth. He is the perfect revelation of all that You are. By living here among us, Jesus understands what it means to be your revelation in humanity. But I also embrace that I am made in Your image, and in embracing this, I acknowledge that who I am brings glory to You. I pray today that I would grow into full maturity in who You created me to be, and that in this, Your glory would be revealed within me. I am who I am for the sake of Your Glory—let all the glory be Yours, in and through me."

To interact with the author and other friends on many of the subjects in this book, “Like” the Facebook page:
https://www.facebook.com/UnspokenGospel/